To

Wendy

Do what you feel
Now as you move
along

Take Care

SPIRITUAL EXPERIENCES

by Bill Harrison

This book is dedicated to
Mrs Dorothy Matthews of
Gloucester. Born in 1916
youngest of 18 children.
A Healer, Medium but most
of all a Friend. A lady
who has given so much,
but in return, has asked
for nothing.

Without the knowledge she
has given to me, I would
not have been able to write
this book.

First edition 1993
© Bill Harrison

Corner Cottage
Hozzard Lane
Blackford
Wedmore
Somerset BS28 4UT

Book Design and Illustrations: Tracey Grist

ISBN 0 9520829 0 X Paperback
     0 9520829 1 8 Hardback

British Library Cataloguing in Publication Data
Spiritual Experiences
A CIP catalogue record for this book is available from the British library

Typeset by Avonset, Midsomer Norton, Bath
Printed in Great Britain by The Fairwood Press, Westbury, Wiltshire.

CONTENTS

PREFACE

This book has been written, hopefully to help others. Throughout my experiences I have realised too many people do not understand the fundamental basics, even some of the Mediums I have met didn't think to ask spirit, 'why?' simply because they didn't know they could.

By sharing my experiences and knowledge with you, I hope I will help shed light on questions you have, but more importantly give you an understanding of healing and spiritualism.

Simplicity itself is as important as anything, you don't need a brilliant mind, you don't need to be rich or famous to be a worthwhile person, you don't even need these goals to better yourself, ordinary people with ordinary jobs doing ordinary things are what it's all about.

Everyone I feel has some gift within, it just needs bringing to the surface, OK, time, patience and discipline play an important role but we wouldn't appreciate anything if it was given to us on a plate.

By helping one another we help ourselves, it is important to care for and to love ourselves as much as anyone, if not more, we do need to recognise this even if we cannot accept it, but remember, this has nothing to do with egotism, how can we accept someone loving us, if we do not love ourselves?

All the views and ideas I express within this book are my own, they are what I believe, none of the associations I am with play any part in my views, therefore this book just contains one ordinary man's opinions, you as the reader should know this, and choose what you want to accept or disregard, it is your own feelings that count.

By writing this book there are many things I have learnt, it has also helped me to understand and it has also shown me what I can and cannot say, my views have been stifled, but then again the truth does hurt, maybe a bit too much!

I hope this book will be useful to your development and understanding.

Do try the exercises out for yourself which are mentioned within, don't be afraid of what you may or may not feel as every one of us is different.

Please enjoy the book.

Bill Harrison

Since the dawn of man there have been those gifted to relieve their fellow men from pain and suffering, to restore normality to the afflicted and contentment to the disturbed.

From every corner of the World, in every culture and creed, there are many authenticated accounts of miraculous cures simply by the laying on of hands. To most who have experienced or witnessed such phenonoma there is awe, astonishment and incomprehensible mystery. To the remainder of us, because these miracles have no earthly explanation, they are generally viewed with scepticism and disbelief.

That they do occur is unquestionable, but in the main these instant miracles are the exception. What goes relatively unnoticed, in many cases even with unawareness, are those healing touches which give relief in a gradual, more progressive and less discernable manner by the many amongst us who have this remarkable capacity to heal. Irrespective of whether their touch be miraculous or progressive, these people are the human channels of the wonderful healing energy of Spirit. An energy that can bring comfort, relief or normality to those in any form of distress.

The nurse whose presence can inexplicably ease a patient's discomfort (specifically recognised in U.S.A. hospitals as Therepeutic Touch Nurses); the mother who can instantly soothe a child; a visitor that can leave a sick relative or acquaintance strangely comforted, who has not on some occasion consciously felt a sense of upliftment from a simple handshake? Many in the medical profession readily admit that they have witnessed such events that cannot be resolved by 'sympathy and reassurance' alone.

Such is the power and mystery of 'Spiritual Healing', a wonderful restorative energy that can be channelled in lesser or greater degrees through chosen individuals. Away from the carnival and hysteria of the much publicised atmosphere of Faith Healing – repugnant to those with true knowledge – there are many who are proved servants to this power and who have an understanding of its source. In all walks of life and occupation, they work quietly and unobtrusively using their gift of the 'Laying on of Hands', mostly without consideration to their personal inconvenience or to their purse.

This is the story by one such Healer, told truely without adornment or embellishment – May it make some of you more aware of the existence of forces beyond our earthbound lives – May it make some of you begin to question our limited knowledge of what lies beyond – At the very least, may it make some of you think.

Joe Wignall, Somerset

Although I only met Bill Harrison a short time ago it seems like I have known him most of my life, because of the way he has helped and taught me.

During the few months I have known him, I have helped him with this book, by illustrating the text, due to this we have had to work through the book together, I found that not only was I helping him but he was helping me by teaching me about the world of spirit and answering my many questions which I have always been afraid to ask just in case I was ridiculed for not knowing anything, he explained his answers in an understandable form, keeping his views simple, I found that not only could I relate to his answers, I could see the sense they made, he didn't go too 'in depth' as many books and people do, he showed me in a way that I would understand, which to me is important.

By reading the book and talking to Bill, it slowly dawned on me how important I am, little, ordinary me, I am entitled to accept what I want, I do not have to believe in everything I am given, and most importantly, I have every right to query what I do not understand.

So many people and religions do not let you have your own opinion, you must conform to their beliefs, but through reading this book I have been shown that, yes I do have the right to speak if I want to.

By reading 'Spiritual Experiences' I have realised that spiritualism is not a one-day-a-week religion, it is a way of life.

Tracey Grist

ACKNOWLEDGEMENTS

I wish to thank my many friends who have made this book possible; friends from the earth plane and the world of spirit.

To Julie Stevenson and Hillary Hoyle who helped by typing my manuscript.

To all the people whom I have met on my travels.

To Tracey Grist for all her help putting the book together and for the illustrations and cover.

My good friend Joe Wignall for all his help and support.

I also wish to express my gratitude to those who have kindly permitted me to include them in this book although the names and other identifying features have been changed to allow them their own privacy.

Thanks to my sister Wendy and the rest of the family for believing in me, but mainly to my sons, Sean and Steven for being there.

And not forgetting you for buying it. I hope you enjoy reading it as I enjoyed the many experiences within it.

FRANCE

CRETE

CYPRUS

Where Bill has travelled in search of knowledge

CHAPTER ONE

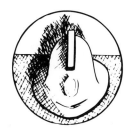

PHILLIP

My story begins in September 1983. I had just moved from Clevedon, a small town in Avon to a smaller village in Somerset which wasn't far away. After living in Clevedon for some 7 years I had made many friends. One of these friends was a young man called Phillip Jones. He was 28 years of age and worked in a local cake factory. His mother and father had passed away several years before, so he lived on his own. Although Phillip was slightly retarded. It did not stop him from getting out and about in Clevedon, and many people knew him as they used to see him on his bike cycling around. When I first joined the Fire Service in Clevedon, I spotted him on his bike as he used to follow the fire engines everywhere they went. When a bleeper or siren went off to tell us of an emergency, we would always shout to Phillip that there was a fire call, he would switch on his large portable radio (that he always carried) and would follow us on his bike. During the time I lived there I used to invite Phillip to my home and the Fire Station, where he talked with all the firemen, and everyone of us knew he was really keen on the Fire Service.

On September 18th 1983, just after I moved to Blackford, I received a phone call to tell me Phillip had passed away, I was very upset after hearing this as I thought alot of him and had many fond memories of Phillip, one of these was when I left the Fire Service in Clevedon he bought me a little silver tankard and presented it to me, this kindness brought tears to my eyes for many days after his passing. Not long after the phone call a voice from spirit said to me that I had to go to Church, the only Church I could think of was a Spiritualist one. I had been aware of the spiritualist movement from a very early age even though I had not bothered to go for many years.

I arranged with the firemen at Clevedon that we would carry Phillip at his funeral, they would wear their uniforms and would bury him as a fireman. This took place a week after he had passed away, it was a very sad and emotional time. Six firemen carried Phillip into a packed Church, even the local Policemen were outside the Church in their uniforms to say a last farewell. The service was very moving and there were many tears shed that morning. Phillip was then taken to a Church near Poet's Walk on Old Church Road, where he was finally laid to rest. One by one the six firemen (including myself) saluted Phillip in a final farewell. The feeling within myself that I must go to Church was even stronger now.

I looked around my area for a Church but couldn't find one, in desperation, I contacted the local police station in Weston-super-Mare and asked them where I could find a Spiritualist Church. They told me of the Blue Cross Church, situated just off the Boulevard, in Weston-super-Mare, so one Sunday evening, two friends and myself made our way to this Church. The greetings when we entered were very warm and gave us all a nice feeling whilst we sat waiting for the service to begin. That night there was a lady Medium taking the service, when the hymns and prayers had ceased she demonstrated her gifts by giving out several spirit messages, and eventually she came to me, I can remember the message even now, she said a lady was with me, who had come to thank me for everything I had done for her son and not to worry now because he was alright; he was in safe hands as they were all looking after him. The Medium also gave me a young man dressed in white overalls smiling - I recognised this as the way Phillip dressed for work. There were various other things in the message she told me that evening which I cannot remember at present but, at the end of the message she said to me,

'Are you aware that you have got powers within your hands to heal people?'

I said no to this because at that time I wasn't aware at all of healing gifts; of how we can be used as a spirit channel to help heal people. I was invited to stay behind after the service and talked to the Medium and another lady who was with her. They were giving healing to someone who had been to the service so I remained to watch what these two Healers did, but unfortunately, I did not see or feel just what they were doing could help anyone, so I chose to ignore the advice that I had been given.

In 1988, after a long period of time, I eventually started going back to Blue Cross Church. I was going through a particularly difficult period in my life as I was suffering a lot as someone who had been very close had left me, I felt alone and really low, so I made my way back to the Church.

I like to sit at the back of the Church away from everyone and I think, now if they want to come to me to give me a message, then they are going to have to find me. So there I was, at the back of the Church behind everyone, head down and back to the wall, sure enough they found me, spirit has found me on many occasions when my morale and feelings are really low. They have come to me with messages and proof of life after death, they have told me about the healing powers that I had, this has been said on many occasions. I do not, of course, get a message every time I go to Church, even so, I find it nice just to sit there and listen to other people getting messages and see the joy on their faces when they are being given proof from the other side. I also like to listen to the philosophy the Mediums give out.

During the next few weeks I received many messages when I went to Blue Cross in Weston or the Dukinfield Church in Greater Manchester (as I would go to this Church whilst visiting my parents). I also found another pleasant Church in Hyde, Cheshire.

During the course of the next few months, spirit also told me not only had I the powers to help people by using my hands, but I was writing a book. Now, I could not accept this 'writing a book' business at all, and yet they told me in each of these Churches that this was what I would eventually do.

One Sunday morning, whilst reading a Sunday newspaper, I noticed a Psychic Course advertised, which was to take place at Hayling Island in November 1988.

I contacted the name and address in the paper and booked myself on this course this was to change my life, there were various people on this course - Clairvoyants, Numerologists, Astrologers, Tarot Card Readers, Graphologists, Palmists, a Reflexologist (who was also a Healer) and many others. When I arrived on the Monday lunch-time I was met by the organisers Pat Dickie and Beryl Lambert (who were running the course for that week). The course was to take place in a Holiday Camp on Hayling Island, it was very peaceful, quiet and refreshing, so you could afford to wind down, which seemed the ideal place to run a course like this. One of the first people that I met as I was queuing up for lunch, an hour after I had arrived was Lorraine Davies, a Graphologist. She was a very warm and caring person, (as you continue to read my book, you will find that she comes into my life at various times and helps me). I built up a friendship with Lorraine and a lady named Marie Wakeling (who was a Clairvoyant) and a few others that week. The course was to cover many aspects of spiritualist work and on the Tuesday afternoon we had a talk and demonstration on healing by Rodney Peacock, after this, we had the opportunity to see what we could do, how we could give healing and how we felt whilst 'giving' it to various people (who were also attending the course) in need of healing. I had the opportunity on this day of giving healing to a very nice old lady called Kittie, from London.

Rodney had talked to us, and discussed the aspects of healing and what we had to do (this was the first time I had done touch healing). There were twelve people that required healing. These people sat on chairs in front of the class and twelve people who wished to become potential Healers, were given the opportunity of coming up and standing behind the individuals, placing their hands on the shoulders of those concerned and letting spirit use them as an instrument. This healing session took between 20-25 minutes and I soon discovered that I could actually feel this lady's pain within my body, this was very strange to me; I could not understand how it was possible to feel somebody else's pain from their body in mine. The types of pain I felt were quite excruciating at times, pain within my shoulders and my neck, within my arms, my hands and within my head. All these pains I afterwards discovered, this lady feels herself and when I talked to her about how she felt after the healing, she said,

"it was lovely, you have drawn all of my pain out of my body just by simply placing your hands on my shoulders!"

I didn't get the opportunity to give healing again until the Thursday. This time the session had dwindled down to some five people requiring healing and five people who were either existing Healers or people who wished to become Healers. Again, I wanted to carry on learning about healing. This time I had a young man sat in front of me, and again, all I did was place my hands on his shoulders, but after a few minutes I discovered I wanted to move my hands onto the back of his neck and head, for some 15-20 minutes I kept my hands on him to give him healing, and again, I experienced pain in various parts of my body which was hard for me to understand, the pain I was experiencing was quite strong, again I was feeling it in my neck, head, but also in my shoulders and my sinus's. Afterwards, when I chatted to the young man, he said to me words that I will never forget,

'I have been a Healer for 9 years and I have never experienced power like you've got, not only were you drawing out the pain from my neck and my head, but I've had problems with my sinus's and you were literally drawing this out through the back of my head to your hands'.

Of course this made me feel very pleased and chuffed, he then went on to Rodney to talk about it.

During this week, I had several readings from Mediums (or Clairvoyants as we will call them). I would like to tell you about them; on the Tuesday morning, I went to see Lorraine Davies, who is a Graphologist (a person who reads handwriting), this is her profession, she also works as a Medium and serves many Churches and organisations around the country and abroad. In the reading she told me of various things, one of these was about one of my guides.

A guide is a spirit that had chosen to be with you and to guide you through periods in your life, our guides often change and don't remain with us forever and a day, as we develop, our guides also develop, along our pathway they change to suit our needs. The guide Lorraine talked about was a man, he was to play an important role in my story. This was the first time I'd been told about him, she said she could see him with me, and he was a member of the Church, not an ordinary Lay member, but a Bishop or something like that, she said, as she continued to describe him that his name was Thomas, but that was all she could give me, she said if I went to Tintern Abbey and looked for Thomas I would find him on a brass rubbing (this idea was then implanted into my mind). Afterwards I saw a lady called Pat Prior-Burnett, now Pat is a Palmist, and she read my palms. That morning I went out and bought a tape recorder and decided that from that date, whenever I could, I would record any messages given to me, no matter where I was I would take a recording as I believed that this would be important to me at some stage (although I didn't know why). After Pat had read my palms and predicted various things, she asked me if she could take a print of both my hands, this was done by applying ink on them and then pressing them onto paper.

She said, 'I always take famous people's prints and then, when we meet again, later on in life, I compare their palms as they are now and as they were when I first took them'.

This put something into the back of my mind then, why did she say something like this to me? - Who knows?

Marie Wakeling gave me a message one night when we were having an evening demonstration of clairvoyance, (but I have to admit I forgot to record it) and yet the message was significant and helped me at that time. I knew, following that November week at Hayling Island, I would eventually meet Marie again and some of the others during my journey. I returned from Hayling Island feeling on top of the world, almost as if I was floating on a cloud, so during the next few weeks, I began visiting Spiritualist Churches in other areas. To see what feelings I felt towards the Church - was there a welcome in the Church? Because, to me, the welcome you get when you're walking into a Church is as important as its atmosphere. It is vital that you get that nice friendly greeting at the door, and that you are made to feel welcome, it should make you feel at ease, as many people that enter Spiritualist Churches today are all looking for different things most are very nervous and need to be helped in stages through-out their journey. I would always sit at the back of the Church to watch and listen to just what goes into the service, the music they play, the hymns they sing, and the messages given from the Mediums, are they psychic or spiritual? - can you tell? I've been asked many times to describe the difference between psychic and spiritual and even at that early stage in my development, I knew it was important to tell the difference; psychic to me is a level that anyone can pick up on, how often are you aware of something going on around you although no one has told you, yet you know? If you visualize seven levels, the bottom level is a psychic level, the seventh level is a spiritual level, which is the level everyone of us should be aiming for. It does not matter what we may do in life, as long as we're reaching that spiritual level, and I feel that when we've learnt to reach that seventh level, there will be another seven levels. We may never reach the top no matter how hard we try or how far we develop, occasionally, I would get some form of con-firmation that would tell me that the Medium was giving a spiritual message as opposed to a psychic message, although it may be necessary to give some parts of a message on a psychic level for people to understand, I hope this explanation helps you. Eventually, I got the opportunity to make my way (with my friend Anne) to Tintern Abbey in South Wales, as we approached on the road that makes its way down into the valley towards Tintern, all of a sudden on the right hand side I saw what was left of the large Abbey, with a river running around the back of it. At first we got the impression that there had been a fire, which was what had destroyed it, but when we got closer to look at it in more detail, we discovered that was not what had happened. After the dissolution of Religious Houses - (including Tintern Abbey) Henry, Earl of Worcester took away all the lead from the roofs and all the bibles, causing the buildings to deteriorate the way they have done over the centuries. As we approached in my car, I suddenly got this very strange sensation running through my body, it was like a very cold shiver with goose pimples (we used to say as children, 'someone has walked over our grave'). I continued to get several more of these 'cold shivers' as we approached the Abbey which became stronger all the time but I was not aware of what these shivers were telling me. I had a good look around the Abbey, but I could not find any signs of Thomas, either in the brass rubbings (that Lorraine told me I would find), or in the history of the Abbey. There was just no signs of him at all. So, as we drove away, I was disappointed that I had not succeeded in finding him and felt deflated.

A few weeks later, I had the opportunity to attend a Healing Sanctuary in Kingswood, Bristol, run by Dennis and Doreen Fare. It was Lorraine Davies who put me in touch with them, she told me how well this couple worked and how well they carried out their healing. I managed to attend a seminar run by them, which discussed the many aspects of healing, they said,

"to start healing you must do what we call 'absent healing' for two years, which is when you know of someone who is sick and needs help, whether this is sickness in the mind or in the body. Then what you do at various times during the day or night that suit you is say a prayer, within this you ask for help for these individuals, in order that they may receive that upliftment to remove the pain or suffering that they are going through, and to benefit from the help they are being given."

I started doing my absent healing feeling very keen, not knowing what would happen, but still putting one hundred per cent into it, fully expecting that if this was what was expected of me to do for two years, then I would do it. At this time a friend of mine Allison, was having trouble with her back, so I started sending out absent healing to her, explaining at an early stage what I was doing, although I told her I didn't know what she could expect but I knew she would receive help, within a few weeks Allison contacted me and told me that the pain she had been suffering from in her back had now completely gone. She put this down to me sending her healing, needless to say I felt very pleased with this result.

I bought myself a few tapes of music, one in particular I liked called Tranquility (no doubt many of you will have heard of it). This tape was to play an important role in my process of learning about healing. I used to play it a lot as listening to it made me feel quite relaxed. One day I received a book from Lorraine Davies, called 'Spiritual Healing Miracle or Mirage?' By a chap called Alan Young. The author was an Attorney of Law in America but more importantly, a Healer. This book explained various aspects of healing, the feelings, emotions and reactions between the patients and the Healer, as I read through this book I found by the time I got to the end (which took me a few months), I was also experiencing many of the things he was stating in his book; what he had felt or seen whilst giving healing. I would recommend, if you have the chance to read this book that you do so, and I only hope that it helps you the same way it helped me and gives you more of an understanding about healing and the feelings you get whilst giving.

I carried on visiting Churches, whenever I got the opportunity no matter where they were. I continued to receive messages that confirmed I would write a book on my experiences, and my healing capabilities, I used to just listen and take them in, but I could never fully accept at that moment in time, that this was what would happen. I got the opportunity again to attend another seminar on healing with Dennis and Doreen Fare at their home. This time they introduced us to various healing techniques that Dennis used when giving healing to others. Some of these techniques I liked, some of them I didn't feel were just for me, not that there was anything wrong with them. I just did not feel suited to the technique that Dennis was using at that time. I think it is important to use a technique that you feel comfortable with, whilst giving healing.

CHAPTER TWO

THE DECISION IS MADE

In April 1989, I flew to Crete where I stayed in a small fishing village called Elunda. I joined up with two friends of mine there; Rob and Jacqui and during the week we visited many places on the island together. One that stands out in my mind most of all, is a visit to a smaller island, (situated in the entrance to the harbour). It used to be a leper colony up to 30 years ago. Whilst we were walking around this colony, I felt very emotional, mainly of sadness and pain, it's very difficult to explain the variety of feelings that I experienced as I walked around. I could feel for the lepers, the suffering that they must have gone through the time they were on the island, you could see the poverty, you could almost hear them crying. If the lepers had still been there I would not have returned to England, as I would have stayed with them and tried to help. I felt very strong about this.

In October of 1989, a Medium called Sally Smith from Glastonbury, explained to me that in a previous life I had been a Knight in Malta, who had suffered with leprosy (this explained and confirmed my feelings in Crete). Later on in April '89 I attended summer school which was run for all the Spiritualist Churches in the South West of England. It was held at Pontins

Holiday Camp in Torbay, again this week was to completely change my life forever. On the Tuesday morning I was having a reading with a lady called Mvanwy Jones, a Medium from the Bristol area. During the process of my reading, Thomas appeared again, so I asked Mvanwy,

'what is Thomas's second name?'

and she replied

'Thomas Becket'

This was a terrific shock to me as I'd remembered Thomas from my history lessons at school, and I knew what had happened to Thomas at Canterbury Cathedral. Mvanwy then told me about my healing and about the book I would write but I still did not accept that I would be writing a book.

In the evenings when all lessons had finished, we used to sit down and relax whilst being entertained by various artists that had been employed at the Holiday Camp. That night there was a chap called Mike Carter, an impressionist. Mike imitated many sounds, vehicles, aircraft - you name it Mike can impersonate it, and after a fantastic act (which kept everyones attention), Mike decided to talk to us, he told us that not many years before he'd been very close to death, and met a Healer (who was also a Medium) one night in a Church in the city of Gloucester, and after this chance meeting, the Medium saved his life, not just on one occasion but three, by using her healing capabilities. He told us all this story, it brought tears to my eyes, because he had so much love in this story, love not only from him to this Healer, but the love and affection this Healer, used to help and give healing to Mike to get him better. Without once accepting any monies of any kind for her work, not only the work she did for Mike but her work she did for spirit, serving many people and many Churches. This lady was 74 years old, Mrs Dorothy Matthews. He found Dorothy in the audience and stood her up so everyone could see her, it was after listening to his story and seeing Dorothy that I made up my mind to write my book and I had decided to dedicate it to her even though I had never met her before or heard of Dot before that day, but I was determined

Dorothy Matthews and Mike Carter
Summer School, Torbay

to dedicate my book to her. When Mike got Dorothy up and showed everyone who she was, she was crying because he was showing his gratitude not only to her, but he showed it to everyone in the camp that week. Afterwards, I made my way across to speak to her and I explained that I was going to write a book and I would like to dedicate this book to her. She said she was very pleased and felt over the moon. I also had the opportunity to speak to Mike whom I had never met before, and explained to him about my book, Mike's words were

'yes Bill and your book is going to be a great success'.

I said curiously,

'but how do you know that Mike?'

And he replied,

'because my guides have just told me'.

Mike had used this expression 'guides'. If you remember I touched on it earlier, friends, helpers, guides; we each have our own names for our spirit friends that work with us on a day to day basis, I prefer to call them friends now, as they are my friends. I talk to them and they talk to me so that we both have a better understanding of each others ways. The following day I had another reading with a Medium called Carol Mayers, during this reading she told me that I had now decided to write my book and I will do so.

On the Thursday morning at breakfast, there were three of us sitting at our table talking; Lil, Hilary and myself. (Lilius and Hilary were also from the Blue Cross Church in Weston-super-Mare) and Lil suddenly said to me

'what does "Spiritual Experiences" mean to you? As someone said to me from the spirit world to tell you'.

I explained that now I had my mind made up to write my book and I would need a name for it, I believed that this was the title my book must have, so I thanked her and her spirit friends. This explains, I hope, where the name of my book comes from – such a simple way of communication, 'Spiritual Experiences'. Little did I know at this time, of the many spiritual experiences I would encounter as I travelled along my pathway with all my helpers. The title itself may not sound much at this time, until, as you carry on and read into the book you will understand some of the experiences they've allowed me to share with them and you.

On the Thursday night I had a dream. It was about a young lady I work with at the Airport (I have worked at Bristol Airport for many years), Paddy the young lady was suffering from cancer. She had worked at the Airport for a few years, handling the aircraft working on the apron, which is unusual for a woman to do. Whenever we got the opportunity, we would talk to one another and just before I went away we'd been talking on how she felt because of her cancer, she was in pain and very worried about it, so if we got the chance we would talk about it to see what we could look at to try and help her for the future, I asked her to go and find a Healer to see what they could do to help her. Paddy had been seeing doctors who were giving her treatment, but she needed something else, and within the dream I had of her, I placed my hands on her shoulders to give healing. The dream was so real at this time, that it gave me far more to think about afterwards. I had accepted for two years that I would not do anything else but absent healing, yet within this dream, I was being told that I needed to do something to help this young lady.

I talked to Dorothy during the rest of the week and we built a friendship between us, that would last forever.

I came home from Torbay on the Saturday feeling full of the joys of spring, for myself and for what I had learnt and experienced. I rang Paddy and told her that I had dreamt about her and that I had to lay my hands on her in order to give her the healing she needed, Paddy shocked me by saying,

'yes, I know'.

So I asked her how she knew, confused, as I'd been away for a week, she said that Lorraine Davies had appeared and she was giving a series of lectures and readings at Bristol University, during part of the week I was away. Somehow, Paddy had heard about this and had gone to meet her for a reading. During this

Lorraine had picked up that Paddy needed help and healing, she proceeded to tell Paddy what she had to do; she was to come to me for healing as I was the one capable of helping her, we talked on the phone for about an hour that night and arranged to meet the following evening. When the Sunday evening came around we met and went to Blue Cross Church, Paddy sat next to me at the back (as usual) during the service she kept commenting on me burning her even though there had been no contact between Paddy and myself at all, but she was feeling a

Inside Corner Cottage

warm sensation. The warmth that was coming from my body and reaching hers without the physical touch was part of the healing process, we need to understand, not burning as in the sense of burning your skin or burning your body so that there is a great deal of discomfort and pain, but just a warming sensation throughout. In Paddy's case the right hand side of her body, as I was sat on her right, this continued throughout the service. I was not experiencing anything, the warmth or any pain or suffering, nothing at all. When the service had finished we came back to my cottage and I put on my tape of tranquility (at a very low level), so it formed a background noise, we talked again for a very long time because we did not know what would take place, we also both agreed to discuss everything afterwards; what we felt, what we saw and what we sensed during the healing process. Paddy sat down on the chair and faced my fireplace, which has a large school-type clock above it ticking quite strongly - it gave Paddy something to focus on. She sat with the back of the chair to her right hand side, thus, leaving all the back part of her body clear. I washed my hands before I started and said a prayer, within this prayer I asked for help and to be used as an instrument of healing, so that my friend in front of me would receive help and healing with love and light. I felt proud and privileged that here we (my guides and I) had a challenge. A young lady that was suffering from cancer, who needed help and chose to accept it from us.

We cannot say to anyone that they will be cured by healing. The only thing we can do is guarantee that they will receive help, and this young lady definitely needed it.

I placed my hands on her shoulders, and eventually I felt that she was receiving the healing given. I moved my hands then on to her head for a short period of time, but got the sensation that she was actually blocking healing (but this only lasted for a few minutes). Then she seemed to remove this blockage and the healing process travelled throughout her whole body. That night the healing seemed to take approximately 15 to 20 minutes (you can never say how long it would normally take - you just have to go along with each individual case). I didn't get any feelings, except a slight pain in my tummy. When afterwards we rested she sat on the settee and I held her hands gently with no force for just a few moments while I was talking to her. I then asked her how she felt, had she seen anything, and how did she feel now? I do think it is important that we talk to the people we are trying to help to see what their feelings or fears are. Paddy explained to me that she had felt a terrific glow and a lovely feeling had entered her body and worked its way down from her head to her shoulders. At first she decided she did not want to accept it, so had stopped and blocked it. After a few minutes she changed her mind and began to receive this warm, flowing feeling down the full length of her body. She could see a blue light flowing through her and into her mind, when this light reached her toes it came back up; up through her trunk, into her shoulders, through her head and then it seemed to shoot out of the top in a terrific white light and she felt very peaceful, at ease and rested. This was the lovely explanation she had for it.

After we had finished I washed my hands again. The idea of washing hands at the beginning and end is to create a fresh link, when I wash my hands afterwards I have broken the link and I am ready for a new patient (in a way it is symbolic but it helps me discipline myself whilst giving healing).

The following morning Paddy rang me at work to tell me that where I had held her hands so gently she had blue finger-prints, not bruises, just gentle blue finger-prints. I touched her hands if you remember, not with any force, this was just part of the healing process. She had shown her mother these prints and even her mother could see them on her hands to her surprise.

During the next few weeks Paddy and I met on several occasions so I could give her healing. When Paddy had to go to hospital for radium treatment which, at that time, to be perfectly honest, I did not expect she would need, she told me that what I had done was to give her help and healing to be able to cope with her actual illness and the medical treatment that she would receive. As she was on her bed, being wheeled down to the theatre, she told the nurses that she had been receiving healing and all that she could see at the end of the bed, was me in a vision just waving my finger at her, to show I was thinking about her and sending her healing.

After the treatment, Paddy spoke to the doctor who told her that the area which they had treated had gone down since her previous examination but it still needed treatment.

Two months later I took Paddy for a check-up at the hospital in Bristol, the doctors were amazed, as was Paddy, because they could not find any signs of the treatment they had done. Everything had healed completely. The scars, stitches all signs that she had been operated on and Paddy was very pleased and very emotional at this time – so was I.

In May I got the opportunity of visiting Dorothy Matthews. She lives in a small, well furnished flat in the centre of Gloucester, full of many items that she had gathered whilst visiting churches working as a Medium. Her husband, Alf, had passed away ten years previously. Before this they both had served churches all over the South West of England.

Dot and I chatted for a bit and then all was quiet, eventually, I realised that she had gone into a trance. I had not been aware that Dorothy was a Trans-Medium, a person that goes into a trance. There are various stages of a trance, that I feel, a Medium can go into, which allows helpers and their guides to speak through them. Dorothy allowed her helpers that night to speak to me for $3\frac{1}{2}$ - hours, which I found absolutely fantastic. The feeling I was getting, listening to the different voices or voice that was speaking through her although she did not appear to change to me were enlightening. She was sat upright in her chair, very well disciplined and all these different helpers were talking through her, I will never forget it as long as I live. Unfortunately, I did not have the opportunity to record any of it as it all happened so fast and caught me completely unawares.

This taught me a lesson that I should always be prepared when I meet a Medium, that may give me a message of some description, to carry my tape recorder with me as I am, like everybody else, human, and you do forget things that are given to you. This is why I started my book on tapes in Hayling Island in 1988 with a view to taping all my messages and writing them all down in a book so that I can always refer back to them and here I was with perhaps the best opportunity in my life; Dorothy's helpers speaking to me for all this period of time, and I just did not get chance to record any of it!

Our friendship developed from that time and I have never

seen a Medium to this day, who works like she does, with such love, power and spirituality. Dorothy has never charged anyone for any of her readings or the work she does in Churches, or to the many people she has given healing to and during her life she has reached many people.

What I forgot to say, the day I came back from summer school, I visited my ex-wife, Beryl (we were divorced in 1977, since she has re-married). I went to tell her how I had felt at summer school and what had happened to me, I also asked her to buy me a book, which I could use for my absent healing list. I wanted her to get me this book and give it to me with love in order that I may start writing people's names in it who required healing; names of people I met or names that I would be given by people I would meet on my journeys who needed this absent healing. Beryl brought me my first book that I would use for absent healing, which started in May 1989. In the front she wrote,

'To Bill, Love Beryl'.

Such a simple message yet I felt it meant so much and so I started writing people's names in it as they were given to me.

Before using a book I used to hold people's names in my head which I found hard at times because after about 40 names I found it difficult to remember each person and I was always frightened of missing one out, so by placing all the names I was given into my book I would simply say a prayer asking that each and everyone of those friends in my book would receive healing that day. This saves me the worry of trying to run through each and everyone of the friends I had been given. I would use this method any time during day or night, by saying a short prayer and asking my helpers to give healing to each and everyone. I would ask my guides to give the healing that these individuals required during the period of time between that day and the next often people would tell me that they were receiving absent healing from me, as they could feel it and felt better in themselves. I had to explain to them that it was not me giving them healing but my spirit guides, who were drawing alongside them and giving them the help that they needed, I was just a channel to be used.

I got the opportunity to travel to Tintern Abbey, looking again for Thomas Beckett. Now that I had Thomas's second name I thought it would make things easier when I got there to find out all about him. When I arrived at the grounds of Tintern Abbey I had my signals; goose pimples all down the right-hand side of my body. They were very strong and active whenever I seemed to think about him or ask about him, whether it was mentally or

Tintern Abbey, South Wales

not - I would always get this signal. But there were no signs of Thomas Beckett, no signs at all.

In June 1989 whilst at the Blue Cross Church, for a service one Sunday evening, a Medium called Dorothy Davies gave me a message. Part of this message was in December I would be taking a journey, with my bag packed, but not to worry as I would come home, you will later discover where this journey took me.

She also said a young man, called Graham was with me. Graham had been a very good friend of mine, who had been killed in a motorcycle accident in 1969 in Hyde. He was only 22 years of age and had been killed just before Christmas (he used to work with me in an ICI Factory up North). The message that Dot gave me was Graham had worked with me in his life and he would now work with me again, this time from the world of spirit, to help me in the work that I was going to do. I felt pleased about this, that a friend who had passed all those years ago should make contact again.

There was no way that the Medium could have known about Graham. She could not have even read my mind as I had no thoughts about Graham at that time. Again, it was something to look forward to, as well as proof of survival.

Also in June I travelled down to Eastbourne, on a weeks Union Course. I had made my mind up to try and (when the course had finished) make my way to Canterbury Cathedral to look around to see if I could trace any signs of Thomas, or if I could have any feelings that would help me understand more. I needed this information to help me know the pathway I was on, so I could understand my friends, helpers and guides that were working with me and using me.

On Thursday evening the tutor had to go away so our course suddenly came to a halt. This gave me all of Friday to travel to Canterbury Cathedral.

When I got to Canterbury I looked all around the Cathedral for several hours. Firstly at where Thomas had allegedly been assassinated, I looked at all the various points and articles which were around the Cathedral but did not get any feelings at all from it, nothing to confirm that Thomas was with me - no goose pimples, no signals of any description.

Whilst I was there I bought a small Canterbury Cross on a chain. Anyone could buy the crosses from the small shop within the Cathedral. For some reason I had decided to buy one.

On the Saturday morning I visited a local Spiritualist Church in Eastbourne, where I met two Mediums, one was a Mrs Dorothy

Gray, who was a nice old grey-haired lady, who I discovered was also a Trans-Medium (with a guide called Amuta). As she began talking to me within the reading she produced various pieces of evidence and asked me to come back to her home during the following week and talk to her, so I explained that I was going to Brighton for a Transport and General Workers Conference and would not be able to guarantee that I could make it.

But on the following Wednesday night, 28th June 1989, I managed to make my way over to visit her, I talked to Dorothy for some 2½ hours, the majority of this she was in trance with her guides and helpers talking through her, explaining many things to me, what sticks out in my mind more than anything was one of the first few facts that she was to tell me. She said she had waited 24 years for me to turn up and had something in the house for me which would be given to me when the time was right. She said I would eventually meet her again and she would give me whatever it was that she had been saving all these years.

She told me that I would devote my life to Spiritual Healing, that I had come with many questions which she proceeded to then give me the answers to, in fact most of these questions were replied to before I'd actually asked them! She also said that I would put pen to paper and write a book that spirit would help me with and lead me to information that I would need. I was also to develop psychically as a Medium, from that day onwards I must always have the best as I insisted I would only accept the best people to train me, as it is so important when you are helping people that you put everything you've got into it - your feelings, dedication etc. Dorothy explained that I would be amazed at my development and I would train people; words would be put into my mouth that would not be mine, in order to talk, help and train other people to make them more aware so they too could understand the spiritual work that is carried out everyday, all around us.

She told me to develop my absent healing as this would become much stronger, especially with contact during the physical process of healing.

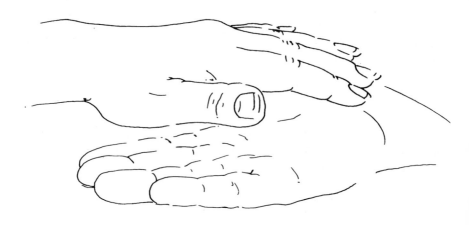

*Begin to feel other peoples energy, first by using just one hand,
then both, recognise the different energies ... who feels what?*

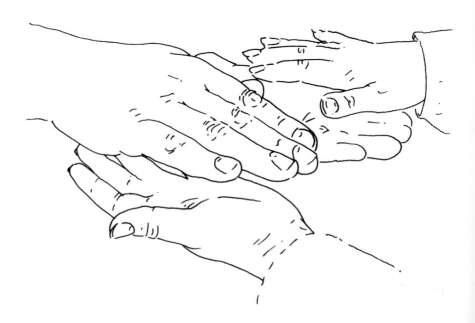

She also told me about cosmic energy that would come from the palms of my hands. Sometimes it would be hot, sometimes it would be cold, different people that I would come in contact with and give healing to would experience this energy although I do not feel anything out of my hands yet so many others do. If you try a simple experiment with your friends, don't touch hands, keep your hands about two inches away from your friend's hands. Put your palms above one anothers palms, without touching and keep them there for a few moments and see what you can feel from your own hands. See what you can feel from your friend's hand as well. Notice this energy yourself, sometimes it's hot, cold, like a static or pins and needles, sometimes nothing at all, but don't worry.

Dorothy also explained something that had been bothering me for many years, as one day in the fire station at Clevedon, whilst a function was taking place, we had a lady reading palms. She read nearly every fireman's palm that night who were attending the station, but when I gave her mine she could not read it. This I didn't understand and I needed it explained. The answer was simple, whatever was in my hand she was not capable of understanding.

She also explained that in a previous life I had been a Monk, living just North of York. She said that I would also write a book on my development and would speak of my own experiences and others whose lives I had come in contact with, and spirit would also help me to write another book.

By the time I came back from the week in Brighton I felt really excited, as if I had gone into another gear to motivate myself.

Notes and Feelings

Chapter Three

Signals of Confirmation

On the 1st July I went to Gloucester to pick up Dorothy Matthews, as she was to conduct a service at the Blue Cross Church, Weston-super-Mare. This turned out to be a great success, as she reached many people who attended the Church that weekend.

During this time Dot stayed in my cottage, and again she went into trance to give me a message, but this time I recorded it. The very first thing that she said was Phillip was here with me again (Phillip who was right at the beginning of this story). She also told me that I had been to Canterbury and, one day I would visit Salisbury and other large Cathedrals. She also said that soon I would be treating someone who suffered with ulcerated legs and I would also set up my own development groups at home, in my own Healing Sanctuary and Alf, her husband (who had passed away), had been with us on the journey today. He had sat with us in the car and it was funny, because as I drove through the village of Wedmore I mentioned about King Alfred who had allegedly burnt the cakes, but could not understand why I mentioned it. Dorothy explained to me, that it had been Alf who had put this in my mind, just so I could say his name.

A few days later, whilst working on this book (using Dot's recording) the phone rang, it was a friend of mine from work who lived in Budleigh Salterton (some 70 miles away), regarding his daughter who was suffering with problems in her legs. I asked him to hang up and I would contact him as soon as possible.

When I switched the tape back on, within a minute I came across the point where Dorothy told me I would be treating someone with ulcerated legs, she had explained what I must do to help them - I would need to put my hands on the person's legs who was suffering, and draw them down three times, in order to help that individual, so I rang the man back and a few days later I had the opportunity to go to Budleigh to see this young girl, I proceeded to give her healing in the method that Dorothy had instructed. I also played my tape of tranquility as background music to put the girl at ease, I moved my hands, touching her legs and feet three times making a flicking motion afterwards as if I was 'dumping' whatever it was I had picked up off her legs, this young girl had been suffering with these ulcers since she had gone to Spain earlier on in the year. She was under the doctor and a specialist but they were unable to find out exactly what the trouble was, her legs had black spots underneath the skin all over, it did not look very pleasant and of course it affected the young girl herself. Again, I didn't feel pain or anything similar with my legs, but I knew that this young girl would receive help and sure enough within 24 hours I had a telephone call from my friend to tell me that the ulcers had almost all gone from her legs. She just had small traces around her ankles left.

I rang Dorothy up immediately in Gloucester to tell her and she told me to make sure that this girl did not come in contact with any water on her legs for a short period of time, as, if she did, the illness would come back.

I rang my friend again in Budleigh to warn him but it was too late. His daughter had gone swimming and the problems had returned. So a week later I visited her again and gave healing, I found that I had to do this on two more occasions following which it cleared completely. She went back to see the specialist and they were impressed with how it had cleared up although they did not understand why. I don't believe that to this day she told them that she had received healing.

She can now go in water whenever she wishes - as it was just for a short period of time that she was restricted, so she enjoys her swimming like every other girl would.

I visited Churches when I got the opportunity and began to realise what I was getting whilst in the service was what I call my confirmation signal or my spiritual signal, when a Medium had given a message that was spiritually true I would get a signal, this signal would come in the shape or form of a cold shiver, goose pimples either down one side or all over my body. This signal told me whether a message was spiritually true or not. Everyone gets some form of signal or another. This is just one of my signals. You too, may be getting that signal similar to me or you may experience some other signal - as if someone is touching you, stroking your hair, face or even the eye twitching. There are so many ways in which we can receive our signals, I would like you to look for them as you go along your pathway.

During the next few months I met many Mediums, I saw Lorraine Davis again a few times (and received various types of messages) towards the end of July, Dorothy Matthews came down again for a weekend, she told me that Alf was with me to assist me with my healing and would like to join my 'team', as Alf was also there to help me develop my Psychic and Spiritual Healing gifts.

We all have our helpers, that work with us, each one does their own job whilst with us; they teach and protect us as we go along our journeys in our way of life. We have someone with us who is called a doorkeeper - a gatekeeper some people may call them, their job is to give us protection no matter what we are doing or where we are, as protection is very important. But we need to make our doorkeeper aware that we need it, this can be done in such an easy way within a prayer:

Please give us protection today and every day,
protect my home, my family and friends,
my animals and myself.
Thank you.

This is such a simple prayer yet we can get so much help
when we say it. It can be said in your own way, with your own
words whenever you want to, as I don't believe there is any
particular time we need to say it although I try to say it every day
as that is what I think is important.

One day in June I'd been to Blue Cross for some healing. The
session I attended was being taken by Edna and Les, Healers
who had worked in the Church for quite a few years. They
conducted themselves in a very pleasant way, they were very
precise and put a lot of thought and love into their healing. I sat
on the stool with Les standing behind me and Edna in front.
Whilst they were giving healing I became aware of another set of
hands actually touching my body, I discovered afterwards that
these hands were actually spirits but with me having my eyes
closed whilst receiving healing I did not know. I was shocked
and amazed to find out afterwards that they had been spirit
hands laid on me, this was the first time I had ever experienced
such a thing, this again made me more aware of some of the
many things that go on around us every day.

About the same time I was at work one day in the kitchen,
with a fellow fireman and he said to me,

'these cobwebs'.

I thought, we haven't got any cobwebs here as the kitchen
was always clean and tidy. So mentally I asked spirit if it was
them and they said,

'yes it is.'

This is how, quite often, they draw close to make us aware by
touching our face, how many times have we had this happen to
us, where we have felt these cobwebs, whether it is in our
homes, our work place or actually out in the fresh air? I would
think and estimate that a good 90% of those times it is not a
cobweb but actually spirit drawing close to us, to make us more

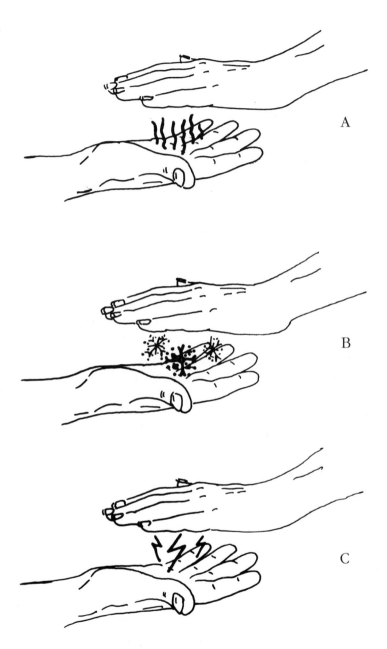

*All energies are different; sometimes we may feel
A, heat B, cold C, static*

aware. I actually received my confirmation signal (as I call it) – my cold shivers – to confirm what was spiritually true.

During the next few weeks I had various people come for healing and realised that they needed some way of winding down whilst I was conducting the healing, not only for themselves but for me, and I found the tape of tranquility which I would play at a very soft level became useful to help people relax. Before the healing process began I would wash my hands before healing to break away any links that I had had before and also to ensure my hands were clean, showing the person that I was giving healing to, that not only have I got enough thought to give them help but enough consideration to be clean, which is very important. A Healer should always be clean, smart and respectable. There is nothing worse than being in close contact with someone that smells of body odours!

I would then say a small prayer, asking the spirit to help me and the individual. At first, throughout the sessions I used to think,

'I want to help this person and this person must be healed',

but after a time I realised that whilst these thoughts were in my mind I was actually blocking the healing I wished to be put forward to that individual, and again, I found that by using my tape of music I would blend into it which helped me to relax. I would talk to the individual who required the healing first, explaining just what is required of them, (as healing is a team effort). That also spirit was using me to reach the individual that required the healing. I explained to them what I would do; where I would touch them and on what parts of their body. I prefer not to ask what is wrong with them as I believe it is the spirit working with you, that will enable you to find out what is wrong with that individual. At times I may feel their pain or sense the problem, or even see the body as a skeleton with the problem area apparent, other times my hands 'instinctively' go to the problem area. The people receiving healing feel hot or cold from my hands, or a form of static electricity as this varies from person to person.

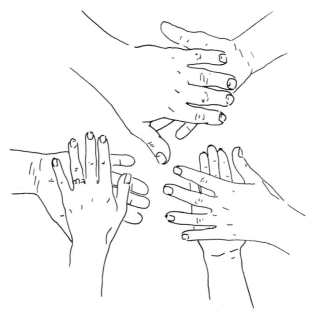

*Get a group of you together and see how the person to your
right's energy is different to that on your left.*

I would start by standing behind the individual and placing my
hands on their shoulders. They would be sat in front of me,
preferably on a stool (giving me easy access to their back). I would
move my hands, when ready, from their shoulders, to their back
covering all the areas. In a way it was like different patterns either
up, down, across or in circles, totally covering their back. I find
there is no need to manipulate or put any pressure on, just gentle
touching of hands. I would move my hands then to the head with
one hand on the forehead. (Normally my right hand as it 'gives
out' healing) and the other on the back of their head. I would
sometimes cover this with movements of my hands. Each time I
would see how long I needed to have my hands in that area, and
spirit would then guide my hands from their head back to the
shoulders and move two fingers on my right hand to just below
the adam's apple with my left on their back. During the process of
this healing you would normally find that the patient was suffering
from stress, as in todays way of life so many of us suffer from

stress, these signs are normally found located in the top part of the shoulders and back, I found that with healing you can normally feel it being taken away and they, too, would tell you how different they felt afterwards.

During healing, as each movement takes place it is not possible to say how long you must hold your hands there for. You just wait, spirit moves you on as they know when it is time to move on to the next stage.

I would then place my hands, one on the tummy and one on the back, again, for no particular time period. I would then move around to the front of the individual in a clockwise direction (to discipline myself) along each arm and leg, I would bring my hands three times to the ends of their fingers or toes and then do a 'dumping' motion where I seem to be literally dumping whatever I have drawn out. By carrying this out three times I felt it would cover all the areas necessary. I would hold just behind the ankle (as this is a trigger point) for a minute or two, to help release the energy that has built up in the limbs. I would then

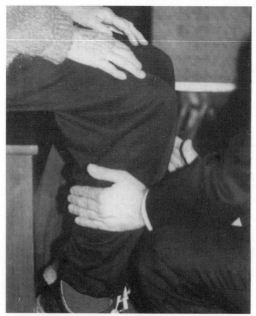

Part of my healing process

move around to the back again, placing my hands on the shoulders. After a few moments, I would step back and I would mentally say a prayer, asking that this person continues to receive healing and help, not only that day but every day.

I would thank my helpers for helping me with this individual and I would bless them, in today's way of life we often don't have time for such trivial things but I find that with healing it is important to find time to say thank you.

I would then place my hands back on their shoulders, on their head and on their shoulders again and bless them. After this I would wash my hands and the healing session would be finished. But I would continue talking to the individual if they needed it. I find it so important to ensure that you continue to have that discipline within yourself whilst being used as an instrument of healing, to ensure that you are always clean and tidy, that your mental thoughts are always correct, you need to be aware. In my terminology I would say there are Healers and there are Feelers, you don't have to undress. There are so many

There's Healers and Feelers

people out there in this world today that are genuinely trying to help others by giving healing, but there are also people who are not doing what they should be whilst giving healing.

If you ever go to a Healer and you don't feel right; something within you is telling you that whatever is going on, whatever is happening, or being said, is not correct, please act on that feeling, do not be afraid to leave. There are charlatans around and you must be aware of them: go on your feelings.

Always be prepared to discuss with the Healer before you receive healing your feelings, what you expect and what the Healer expects, during the session. Get them to explain to you what they are going to do, so you are fully aware of it. It helps you to put your body and mind at ease and in the correct pattern to receive healing. It is important for Healers to talk to the individual first so that they are fully aware of what is going to happen to them. Where you may or may not touch that individual, a person should never be touched in an area that will cause any embarrassment at all, there is no need to do that. You may be an individual that does not like being touched - then OK, all the Healer needs to do is to sit in front of you or near you and talk to you, you will still receive healing that way. You don't have to be put in an embarrassing or awkward situation whilst you are receiving healing. Always bear this in mind.

CHAPTER FOUR

RUNNING WATER

In July, I drove over to Salisbury Cathedral which was about 2½ hours from my home. When I got there I had a good look around and joined one of the tours, what surprised me was that the man who had designed Thomas Beckett's crypt also designed Salisbury Cathedral. This, I felt, was the link I had to find when I visited Salisbury.

Not long afterwards Pam, (a friend of mine) came to my home asking for healing. I gave her healing in the way I explained earlier, she rang me back the day after and said to me that she had not been able to move her arm straight for over 2 years and I told her that whilst I had been giving her healing I had picked up some form of blockage in her elbow. What had happened overnight was that spirit had succeeded in clearing that blockage which was why she could bend her arm straight for the first time in two years.

In August I got the opportunity, again, of inviting Dorothy Matthews down, I always look forward to Dorothy visiting. Not only does she teach me so much, she helps me a lot and is such a lovely friend, a friend that you know you can rely on and talk to, someone that you feel proud to know and in their company always feel relaxed. She came down to stay with me for three days, during this period we had the opportunity of talking a lot, as usual, about her knowledge and wisdom of spirit. One evening, with my father (who was also visiting), my brother-in-law Allan and my sister Hillary, Dorothy and myself formed a circle, during this circle Dorothy and her helpers talked and explained many things.

A circle is when a group of people sit, again disciplined, wishing to learn - to learn from spirit. To receive some form of communication from spirit to help them and others to aid their own individual progress.

One of the loveliest things that happened that night was an Indian spirit talked through Dorothy whilst she was in trance and when he finished he offered us the pipe of peace to share with him (this pipe was, of course, in spirit). He offered to share this pipe with each and everyone of us that sat within the circle, the idea was that we would pass this spirit pipe from one to another and share it with him. This was the first time I had ever been offered such a thing, it was a lovely feeling, one I'll never forget (even though I would be offered it again on many occasions from spirit, as I would go along my pathway) I would always remember this first time. After we passed the pipe and returned it we thanked him for offering us this as a token of friendship to express peace. The Indian was sharing his feelings with ours to show that we were all brothers and sisters together.

In August 1989, I attended a demonstration in a small village hall near Bridgwater. A lady that night called Vanessa, was doing a demonstration of clairvoyance, all the proceeds were in aid of 'DIGIT' (which was a fund that had been set up to save the gorillas).

Throughout the night I watched Vanessa give various messages, but I could not make up my mind whether she was reaching a spiritual or psychic level.

The following weekend I managed to attend Dennis Fares in Bristol for another healing course and seminar. Various things were discussed that day and I found that I had learnt a lot as well as making several new friends.

Following Vanessa's demonstration I got her phone number

and decided to give her a ring to see if I could visit her. To my surprise I discovered that she actually lived near Birmingham, which of course, was nowhere near my home. But, in September I managed to travel up there so after I had finished my shift that day, I made my way to Vanessa's house.

The journey took me 2 hours and when I arrived at Vanessa's she gave me a reading, a reading is when you meet a Medium or a Psychic that will give you various points of information and proof of survival, this can last from ten minutes to an hour or even longer at times. She told me that I would be helping a man who had a drink problem and asked me what I thought about this. I replied, that it was normally self-inflicted but nonetheless, it is an illness that people need help with.

Vanessa also told me of a young lady shedding many tears. She asked me if I knew who she was as I would be helping her as well, but I didn't know of anybody.

She also told me that I would have my own Sanctuary one day, and that the music I will use would play an important part in it.

Following this reading I realised that Vanessa was reaching that spiritual level and was capable of giving spiritual messages and not just psychic.

On the Friday, I travelled up to Dukinfield to visit my parents, as I had planned a journey that would take me about a week. That night I had the opportunity of going to a Church with my father. This was the first time I had been to a Spiritualist Church with my dad for a long time. It always seemed to me throughout my life that dad had always been interested in spiritualism. I can remember as a kid he used to hold circles in our front room, although I was never allowed in, I just used to see people coming and going on a Saturday night. I also used to travel with my dad to a little Spiritualist Church in Dukinfield up to the age of about eleven, my dad had carried on going but I hadn't bothered which I hope explains to you how I knew about spiritualism from a very early age, as I had always been brought up with it. Anyway, when we got to the Church which was a prefabricated, single storey building, situated in an area built up of terraced houses, where the doorstep literally is on the pavement. We sat outside the Church in the car for awhile looking for signs of life within it. After about 15 minutes we realised that candles were being lit, I thought, 'this is going to be different, a candle lit service', I wondered if it would be more spiritual, but when we went inside the Church, we discovered that they'd had a fire the previous week which had cut off the electricity, so the candles were to give us light for the service, the Medium that night was a man called Eric (it was also his responsibility to run the Church), at first when I sat down I couldn't relax due to Eric having a small, scruffy looking dog, which was running in and out of the Church; in through one door and out the other. There was also a fire door which kept flapping about in the wind, as no one was capable of closing and locking it because it was twisted, but after a few minutes desperation took me and I managed to shut it. I noticed at the same time there were many black plastic bags around full up with various items (for a jumble sale to be held in the Church as soon as the electric was put back on), needless to say I thought 'what have I come into and what's going on!' The service began with hymns and prayers then Eric started demonstrating his mediumship, he came to me with a small message during the service, within that message he asked me if I was giving healing and how far I was prepared to go with it. He told me never to back out, never let anyone turn me against it and proceed full steam ahead. Before the service had finished, Eric asked me to give him healing, this was very unusual as this happened actually within the service itself, I'd never known it happen before (and haven't seen it since), Eric in fact, turned out to be the man with the drink problem that Vanessa had predicted. Following this, a couple of ladies asked me to give them healing as well.

On the Saturday night I got the opportunity of visiting a Church in Denton not far away from Dukinfield. This was also in one of the back streets and, as usual, I sat at the back of the

Church and watched the lady Medium give a demonstration, I did not seem to gain much knowledge from her but I noticed something else and when the demonstration had finished, I asked a young lady who was sat next to me, why do you desperately need to talk to someone? She told me how she felt suicidal and said she had many domestic problems at home that had made her feel this way. I talked and explained many things to her; how to talk and communicate with spirit, how to ask for help for herself as I knew this would help her. I knew that spirit was helping her and they would continue to do so through the many days that followed. That night when we parted the girl felt a lot better and looked a lot better, and I felt pleased that spirit had given me a task like this one to perform, I also felt that this was the girl who Vanessa had told me about in the previous week.

On the Sunday afternoon, my father and myself went to visit a small Church in Hadfield, which is situated on the edge of the Pennines, what a beautiful feeling you get when you enter that Church! This again, was a single storey building about fifty metres long with a tin corrugated roof with the sides also of the same material, it was painted dull brown on the outside and you wouldn't really notice it if you were walking past, but when you walk inside what a lovely feeling and greeting that awaits you when you enter. The Medium that afternoon was a lady called Ann Allen from Manchester, she gave several messages that afternoon as part of her service, but what stands out most in my mind was during the service a four year old boy walked into the Church, quite unconcerned, in his hand he had a stick, his trousers and underpants were missing completely, but he wasn't too concerned and neither was anybody else, he walked around the Church while the service was taking place and eventually sat down. Also, a cat entered, this also walked around and sat down right at the front as if to listen to what the Medium had to say, all these things just added to that lovely feeling that I felt when I entered this Church, it showed me that everyone was welcome no matter who or what they were. On the Sunday night I went to the Church in Dukinfield again, this is also a single storey prefabricated building, not very large inside but a nice friendly atmosphere, and the people are always very friendly and give you a greeting to make you feel welcome. The seating only manages to accommodate some 60 people, and when I sat down I became aware of a young lady sitting in front of me, soon I realised she had something to tell me, so I just said to her,

'go on then, what have you got to tell me?'

She turned around and said, 'you will find what you are looking for when you hear running water',

so I replied

'who are you then?'

And she told me who she was and that was all she had for me, I said to her jokingly,

'I wish you were coming with me',

she replied,

'no, you must go on your journey on your own, but we will meet again one day'.

On the Monday I continued on my journey and drove up to York, as I intended to spend a few days there looking for something. I had not told anyone what I was doing or what I was looking for. On the Monday afternoon I made my mind up to find the local Spiritualist Church and also find out what was going on that week whilst I was there, in order for me to go and see if I could learn anything, I went to the local Tourist Information Bureau and they told me where the Church was, it was situated on the outskirts of York in a small quiet lane, the building was an old detached house, maybe one hundred years old. When I got there, there was no signs of anyone else around, in front of the door was rubbish and leaves that had obviously been there for a long time, thus I had a feeling that the building had not been used, the windows were dirty and the building itself looked totally dilapidated, almost as if it was ready for demolition. There was no sign of life at all. Opposite the Church were several cottages, I knocked on a few of their doors in order to ask if anyone knew if the Church was still in use, but I did not receive any reply to my knocks, then an old lady appeared walking up the lane,

so I asked her,

'is the Church still in use?'

and she said,

'I think it is',

but I said,

'it can't be, especially with the amount of rubbish that's blown against the door',

and thought right, that is it, no luck this time, and as I started to walk away back along the lane I saw another lady approaching so I thought I have asked, and I have tried and I'm not going to ask again. When the two ladies met up, they started talking, and the second lady shouted me and asked,

'Do you want to go to the Spiritualist Church?'

I answered,

'yes',

York Church

so she explained she had just come from there, as it had now moved around the corner, and would I like her to take me? She took me around the corner to a very large, old Orthodox Church and she told me that a circle was in progress at that time and the walk itself to this Church only took a matter of two or three minutes. When we got there the door was locked but she knocked and a man soon came to the door to answer. The lady explained to him that I'd been looking for a Church and then said goodbye and carried on her way. I walked into the Church and followed the man past the pews and into the Vestry, which was a very small room with a rather large table against the wall. The walls were damp and smelt musty, hanging on them were several huge oil paintings of members of the clergy who had obviously served the Church through the decades whilst it had been going. The man greeted me and made me welcome and I explained who I was and why I had come,

he said,

'yes, but you have done far greater healing than we have ever seen'.

I replied,

'you can't say that my friend, you don't even know me',

but he said,

'yes I can, my guides are telling me about you, that's how I know.'

He then invited me to join them in their group for a meditation. I explained to him that I'd been going to circle for over a year and I could not honestly achieve winding down into a meditation state, but I would try. He talked us into meditation and away I went. It was beautiful, I went into the halls of learning, and met various spirit friends whilst there, this really helped me. I felt over the moon that I had managed to achieve this as I had tried for so long before and got nothing. He asked me if I minded being used to help the others within the circle that day, there were only eight of them and he asked them to look at me with their spiritual eye and to see if they could see what colour light was all around me. He explained that he was teaching them to read auras, which is another gift from spirit; when you can see various colours around the individuals, this then tells you about the person, whether they are ill, or have any problems or even of their personality. When you learn (it takes time to read auras) you can tell all about the individual themselves, just by looking at them and acknowledging what colour or colours are around them. Four of them said that day they could see a pure white light all around me, but I didn't understand it, at the end of the session within the group, I was asked if I would like to close in prayer. The feelings I had were tremendous, it may only seem small to you, but I'd never been given the opportunity to close in prayer, anywhere, and I was overwhelmed with gratitude for being allowed to do it. I was invited back that night for a healing session which was being conducted by a man called Andrew Lang. When I returned that evening, I discovered the session was to be held in the same room. There were more people there this time, people who needed healing as well as several Healers themselves. I wasn't the only stranger that night, there were two young girls who had attended out of interest to see what they could discover about healing. One thing Andrew did do was change the ordinary light bulbs to blue ones, he felt that this blue would help the people with healing (you normally find that if you have a room painted blue or blue within it, it gives you that tranquil feeling). Andrew asked me if I would open up by saying a prayer, I thought how strange this was, I'd never been given the opportunity before and yet twice on one day I was asked to say prayers, during the evening I watched various people receive healing and I was given the opportunity to give some as well. I found this was yet another link that I had made on my journey.

On the Tuesday and Wednesday I walked all around York, looking for something, but I did not find anything at that particular time, on the Wednesday night I attended a demonstration by a man called Graham Nesbitt, who was an International Medium. He had originated from the Newcastle area, if you listened to him talk you could hear his Geordie accent, which some people may find hard to understand.

The demonstration took part in a committee room in York. I did receive a message from Graham, but many of the things he gave me I did not know of, for example, the people, or symbolic things he was telling me, but that night I made contact with another two ladies, these women were drawn to sit next to me, at the back of the room during the demonstration and when it had finished we stopped and had a cup of tea and chatted, quite often this is when you can help one another most by simply talking together. Both of these ladies told me they had suffered bereavement, one lady had lost her husband and the other had lost her son in a tragic motor cycle accident, and they were both having problems adjusting to what was a new way of life for each of them. The three of us talked together on how to deal with these problems. I explained to them how I felt they could ask spirit to help them cope with their own bereavements.

On the Thursday, I travelled to a small Orthodox Church in a village called Pocklington (my father had asked me to go there as he had been based close by during the last world war). Situated at the rear of the Church is a graveyard where there are airmen of various nationalities buried who were killed during the war, the feeling I got there was perfect peace. The graveyard itself was immaculate with tombstones all set out in single lines, obviously they were being well cared for. After my visit to this Church I travelled on to a town called Beverley. I managed to park my car and walk towards a large Minster which I discovered was Beverley Minster. On my approach I noticed an Antique Centre along a narrow street, (I love looking around Antique and Junk Shops so in I went to have a browse). As I was reaching the top floor I could hear running water which made me recall the message that the young lady had given me, and this was the first time that week that I'd actually heard running water, yet I had been looking everywhere for it. The source of the water was a small fish tank with water flowing into it, at that time I received no form of confirmation from spirit to tell me that I had found what I was looking for whilst I was in there. I then went into the Minster itself to have a good look round, and again I had no particular strong feelings of any description. I had travelled a long way to find this particular place, and I was looking for something very special within it, I felt lost actually and disappointed that I hadn't found what I was looking for. So I made my way back to York and on the following day (Friday), I returned to Dukingfield again, over that weekend I visited various Churches in the area and eventually went home to Somerset on the Monday.

Each night I send out absent healing, my list was beginning to build up. I would not only send healing out to my friends and the people in my book but to all the living things all over the planet earth; the plant kingdom, war torn areas, the planet earth itself, all the people that would be suffering sickness and I also started sending out to the animal kingdom.

In the early October, I visited a Church in Bridgwater. A lady Medium that night gave me a message, she told me that St Francis of Assisi was with me at that moment in time. I proceeded to accept this message as only that short while before I had started adding animals to my healing prayers. It is so important that we recognise there are no limits, no distances we cannot cover, no areas we cannot reach within our healing thoughts. Never be afraid to send them to the other side of the world and never be afraid to send them to areas where there is death or devastation, drought, famine or wars. Our prayers are always answered, although, sometimes not in the way we expect.

Again in October, I attended Dennis Fares in Bristol, for yet another one of his magnificent seminars, where again, various aspects of healing were covered, but most of all we could talk and discuss and learn from one another.

On the 22nd October, I found my way to a small Spiritualist Church in the city of Wells (the service takes place in a St Johns Ambulance Headquarters). The Medium that afternoon was a girl called Sally Smith, she conducted herself and her service in a way I had never seen before, after the normal prayers and hymns she started her demonstration, as she began to give her first message, she gave that person a colour – and then explained what that colour meant to that individual. Then, after she had finished giving her message, she asked the individual to choose a colour for another person in the Church and then proceeded with the next person in the same manner and so on. I felt during that afternoon she reached a lovely spiritual level and I liked the way in which she carried out her responsibilities to reach those people in Church. We talked afterwards and became very good friends, friends you know you can rely on, are so rare at times, aren't they?

On the Friday night of the 27th October, I decided to call some of my friends together to form my first group. Bill, Julie, Doug and Beryl (who were from the Blue Cross Church) Hillary, Allan, my sister and brother-in-law, and Lil my friend from Blue Cross (who you may remember from Summer School). I also invited Sally Smith to talk to us. That evening she talked us through meditation and each one of us saw our helpers who were with us at that time, we all saw them spiritually within our mind. This evening was the start of my first ever group and I hope the start of many groups to come.

On the Saturday, I travelled up to Gloucester to see Dorothy Matthews and her daughter June, June had invited me to sit in a circle with them. She is also very capable of being a good Medium and goes into trance (with her helpers talking through her) although she'd not done it for some time now, so that night the four of us sat, June and her husband Brian, Dorothy and myself, one of the messages I received was from my friend Graham again (who had been killed a few years previous in that motor cycle accident). He asked me to go and find his mother, as his mother was still having problems relating to his death. June told me I would travel back to York again, and this time it would be on a train, my immediate thoughts were, I never go anywhere on the train. Various other messages were given to me by different spirits talking through June, it was a most enjoyable evening.

In the first week of November, I met up with Lorraine Davies again in Bristol, and I took her to a small village in Gloucester. Whilst we were travelling there, I told her the story of my trip to

York and what I'd experienced, I was getting to the point of telling her exactly what I'd been looking for, which was that I had been told in a message that in a previous life I'd been a Monk living in the vicinity of York, so I decided to go and look to see if I could find anything at all that would prove it to me. Just as I was reaching this stage in telling her this story, we both saw a large sign by the side of the road that simply said 'A Monk', it had a picture of a Monk on it. I will never forget it as long as I live, this was both mine and Lorraine's confirmation of my story, that I had found the place where I had lived many centuries before, in a previous life. I do believe in previous lives, I believe that we choose to come back when we are ready. We come back to learn each time, we choose our parents and what we need to go through within this life time, in order that we may learn to then eventually pass and go to the spirit world, taking that knowledge with us and where we also remember what we have learned in previous lives. This is something I ask you to look at and think about, if you find you cannot accept it, then, OK, just dismiss it.

NOTES AND FEELINGS

CHAPTER FIVE

THE GOLD RING

For approximately three years, Ive had it on my mind to have some cards printed showing my name and address. For one reason or another, I'd never been successful in having them produced just how I wanted them to be, until I asked a close friend of mine, Allison Stephens, to come up with a design. This she did and I was very pleased with the result and had them produced. So on a Friday in November, I collected my cards from the printers, little did I know at that time, what effect these cards would have on many people.

The day after I travelled to Bournemouth for a Psychic Course (following on from the one I had attended at Hayling Island). During this week I met up with many old friends and made many new ones. Two new friends in particular; Marie Davies, who talked about the aspects of love and explained a lot of things to everyone about caring. The other, was a lady called Shileen Rodgers. Shileen was a very colourful character with bright red hair, a young lady in her thirties, very jolly and friendly, she wore a huge amount of rings on her fingers, the type of jewellery she wore was also very colourful, but a lovely, loving person. As this week progressed I had the opportunity of giving people healing, and I also began handing out my card and telling these people 'simply hold the card and ask for help whenever you need it', whether it was help with a particular problem they had to cope with or whether there was a condition where they needed healing, I told them they would receive the necessary help from my spirit helpers. On the Thursday morning I had a reading with Shileen and she to me reached a very high spiritual level within the reading. She told me that I would have a centre built and she also linked me with people who I knew in spirit and on the earth plane, she also said that I had two questions to ask at the session in the afternoon, and when I asked these questions I would have to be extremely careful, I knew I had these questions all week because I had become aware of people who were suffering from headaches, feeling tired and weak, basically a general feeling of being unwell, but I couldn't understand why, so in the after-noon, at the questions and answers session, I asked my first question,

'why hadn't any prayers been said either before or after any of the sessions that had taken place that week?'.

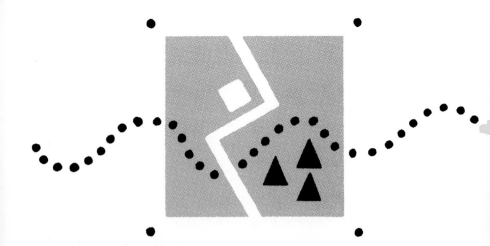

My Healing Card

The female Medium whom I addressed this to simply replied,
'you can say your ***** own prayers',
this shocked me, it wasn't quite the answer I'd expected, but
this naturally made the people there sit up and think, they
became more aware that something was happening which
wasn't quite right. A few more questions were dealt with from
other members of the audience before I felt it time to ask my
next question,
'Why had no protection been asked for during the week, at
any of the sessions?'
I felt the woman avoided answering me straight, so the reply
I received was not satisfactory at all, by protection, I mean, if
you visualise yourself as a battery with a charge, what some
people are quite capable of doing is removing that charge from
us, some may or may not be aware, that they can do this to
others, so what we need to do each day within our prayers, is to
ask our helpers to protect us from such people. For example, if
you are travelling anywhere on public transport or coming in
contact with the general public, you may sit near to an
individual who is quite capable of draining you, so you too
need to be aware that it can happen to you. But unfortunately,
very few people talk about it. I hadn't got over the shock and
disbelief in the way my questions had been answered by this
so-called Medium and when the session finished this same
Medium decided to give us meditation, at the beginning of it she
asked for protection for all of us (this I was pleased to hear),
and built up psychically a large gold ring around the circle. I
found I could actually see this ring, which was amazing because
I didn't normally see things from spirit, as she started the
meditation, somehow she 'zapped' me. My head was forced
down against my chest causing me to feel uncomfortable,
almost in pain, and I realised that the circle of protection that
she had built around us, not only stopped anything from getting
in but it stopped anything from getting out. It was quite
frightening to actually experience, especially knowing that one
person could create a force of that strength.

On the Friday afternoon when the course had finished and everybody was going their own way home, many of the people were still feeling unwell. When I arrived home, I also did not feel one hundred percent, I felt ill in a very strange way which lasted for two days, I soon realised that I was under psychic attack, this happens when one person sends out 'bad thoughts' to another, to either drain them of their power or to make them feel generally unwell. I also discovered that my friends Marie and Shileen were also experiencing the same feeling for about the same length of time. Even my two cats at home reacted, as they knew something was going on, they would not come into the house at all, as they too were picking up a bad feeling, all this time I could see that Mediums face in my mind, this confirmed to me that she was the one who had put me under psychic attack, because I'd actually had the nerve to question her and to challenge her, she didn't approve obviously.

People need to realise that there is a dark side which has developed throughout time, they have passed their knowledge on to one another through the centuries, whereas, I feel, we have failed to do so, we have not communicated with each other, we have not passed on the love and light which needs to be generated and passed on to all mankind.

Witchcraft worries me no matter what heading it comes under, after all, white witches are still witches of the occult and I feel the occult should be avoided at all costs.

People don't realise that witchcraft still exists, they don't know that human sacrifices do go on today, quite often under our own noses! We need to recognise the vibration in an area that witchcraft is carried out, as it is (to say the least) unpleasant and horrific. We must all continue to send out as much love and light as we can, yes, even to those people we don't like!

Around this particular time, one night I had a dream or 'a vision' (whatever you would like to call it), where I'd gone back in time for many centuries to the country of France. I could see someone in a horse drawn cart being taken away to be guillotined, I felt that Shileen and myself had been together in a previous life, and that it was one of us being lead away to be guillotined. I contacted Shileen and explained to her what I had seen within this dream and she also felt it was spiritually true.

How often do you feel that you have been here before in another life? Whether as a man or woman, rich or poor, there are so many vibrations. How often have you gone somewhere and thought you have been there before? You probably have, in another life.

Halfway through November, I went with four friends to see Stephen O'Brien in Bristol, I felt disappointed, as I expected more from such a skilled and experienced Medium, although it may have been the conditions he was working in, or the people in the audience, he didn't appear to me, to reach the spiritual level he is capable of. From the 150 people who attended only approximately 10 people received a message. I expect Mediums working with such a large audience to be capable of working on a faster vibration and reaching more people to keep the interest up but that is only my opinion. The audience should also recognise that they too play an important part, by sending out love and light to the person on the 'platform' as negative vibes even boredom can block the Medium. I do find that the attitudes of the different people in front of us can affect us however we work.

When I talk to people about healing, I always explain that they need to ask for healing for themselves first. It is so important, you are not being selfish, you're just ensuring your charge is always built up. Many of you send out healing to people in many areas around the world, but how many of you actually ask for healing for yourself, either first or within your own prayer? I would like you to think about this because on many occasions we send healing out without even thinking of asking for it ourselves. I believe it gives you a better under-standing by asking for yourself first and realising that you too can accept healing. I would also recommend that within our short prayers we ask for protection for ourselves. We should ask for guidance in whatever we do each day or night, whether it's working for spirit or within our home lives. We ask for knowledge and wisdom from our many spirit friends that draw close, in order that they may help us to understand the many things that we can be given from the world of spirit. I receive lots of messages from Mediums as I go on my journeys and you may feel while you're reading this book, that I rely on these messages to live my life, but this is not true. There are many forms of messages that we can be given, the main form is proof of survival after death, that your loved ones, once they've passed can communicate with you with evidence that only you would know about. It may be their names, it may be the conditions with which they passed with, it may be a happy memory in which you shared with them while they were on the earth plane. There are so many things that can be given to us, we can have materialistic messages that will simply be telling us something that is going on in our material life, and how we can actually cope with it if there is a problem. As we look and listen to the Medium when they give us this message, we must decide ourselves whether or not we are prepared to accept what they are giving us, what I would like you to realise is that many times we are given the names of individuals that are with us that we cannot relate to at that time, and if you think that you've broken down in your car on a road and somebody stops and gives you help, you may not be aware of who that individual is, but they have stopped to give you help, this is what happens when our friends draw close from spirit. They stop to help you because at that time you need their help. Sometimes we are given things within messages that we, for whatever reason, do not want to accept, then OK, lets reject them, there's no need to hold onto them. So many times we can hold onto many things that have been given to us within a message which is absolute rubbish, our minds are already full of this rubbish, so what we have to do every so often is have a good clear out and get rid of this and, if sometimes we throw something away that perhaps we should have held onto, it will be given to us again at another time, in another way, so it makes you remember. Don't ever be afraid of the messages you are given, no matter who tells them to you. Sometimes it may be many months or even years before you remember something that's been given to you in a message, an individual, a happening or something, so don't think you've got to know immediately what it is they are giving you. Personally, I would expect the same type of message to be given to me three times, and I question everything that is given to me, no matter who the Medium is. I always look for signals within my body to ensure that what the Medium is saying is spiritually true.

During November I attended a seminar in a Church up North. This was run by a well known Medium (who will remain anonymous). During the day she discussed various aspects of spiritual work. She told the people of the pathways that she felt were right for them, clairvoyance etc, although she could not pick up at all on me. At the end of the seminar we had a question and answer session,

and I asked her,

'why have you not mentioned protection at all?'

and she replied,

'there was no need for protection',

'but I can assure you there is,' I said,

and thus we had a slight disagreement (lasting nearly half an hour), all those other people at the seminar sat patiently listening and taking it all in, as I believe everyone should ask for protection as I've previously stated. Afterwards as we were all leaving the Church, the lady Medium came across to me and agreed with what I had said, I was right, we do need to ask for protection, but what disappointed me more than ever, was she had refused to admit it in front of all those people who had attended the seminar to learn, and they were the ones who needed to know.

On the 1st December, I drove to Essex to meet Shileen. She took me to a place called Burnham-on-Crouch, we went to look at a new Psychic Shop that was opening that day. A Psychic Shop is where people can have readings and buy various items that are associated with Psychic work. Here I met a Medium who gave me quite a long reading. Within this she gave me a message; she told me I would do healing and travel all over this country and the world. I would talk and explain to many people about healing. She also told me that Harry Edwards was with me, I was pleased about this and felt reassured that such a famous man had chosen to work with me. Harry Edwards was a famous Spiritualist Healer who had his own Sanctuary in the countryside at Shear in Surrey. Harry also travelled all over the world and treated many thousands of people, most of which were cured instantly. He was a kind, gentle man who passed away in 1976, but his memory still goes on to those many thousands of people whom he helped in his life time.

I felt the Medium's message that afternoon was more psychic than spiritual, although she did tell me things that I already knew and that I had to ignore this message for approximately 9 months (as Mediums can tell you to ignore a message until the time is right) for then, I would know and be able to understand it.

On the Saturday I watched Shileen as she worked at a Psychic Fair (you would normally pay to get into a Psychic Fair, then pay for a reading). What was quite apparent to me from the first minute I walked in there was very poor vibrations in the room itself, and when I sat and watched the people working there, I realised they too were on a very low vibration. I wouldn't insult Mediums by calling these people Mediums as they were on a very low psychic level, quite possibly never reaching a spiritual level within their messages. The people that were attending obviously needed help (as that was the reason they had come), but I didn't feel they'd get much help that day from the many people that were working there. I watched Shileen and yes, she did reach people, she did give them proof of survival and evidence which these people needed, but I felt she was in the wrong environment, as her skills far exceeded the others present.

When the day finished, we travelled to Marie's in Watford, to meet her family and various people who were also there. On the Sunday night with Marie and her husband Bert, Shileen and myself were sitting in their flat when I suddenly became very excited as I realised that spirit were with us. I had never felt spirit this strong with me before, and when I went upstairs to get my tape recorder from my room (in order that I could record anything that went on) I knew they were coming with me. I don't know whether it was excitement or fear but the sensation was brilliant. Also there was something I'd never seen before, a small round white light which came with me to my room. When I opened the door of my room I was honestly afraid. I don't know how I would have coped if I had seen a spirit form there, on the other side of it, I suppose you call it fear, even though I knew full well that it would not harm me, it is difficult to explain. I felt that if this light had been magnified hundreds of times it would have looked like the planet earth with the various patterns of the continent on it. Yet this light was only a matter of half an inch round.

I went back to join the group and the light came with me. Bert had fallen asleep and Marie had lit a candle, I discovered that by lighting a candle during a group meditation or discussion, if you closely watch the flame, it reacts in different ways to whatever is being said. If what was being said was spiritually true the flame would grow in height and brightness, just another way of making you aware. Shileen went into trance and various guides talked through her, especially a Red Indian who gave us all feathers and he informed us that one day we would have a better understanding of the meaning of the feathers. He told me that the three feathers would tell a story, all of this time I was still aware of the white light with me. We were also all aware of three spirits being present with us during the evening.

When the sitting had finished the white light completely disappeared and yet the feeling within the room was very calm and peaceful.

I discovered later on in my journeys that if you are given a feather it is a reward, as this is how the Indians used to get the feathers for their head-dresses, for each feather in their head-dress they had to earn it, one way or another.

I am often given a feather within a message but the person giving it to me does not have a clue why they are giving it or what it means. It is just nice for you to know, in case you ever receive a feather in a message.

This journey I had been on to Marie and Bert's had been the one I was given early that year by a Medium (as I have previously mentioned).

My group were developing quite well and we had been joined at this time by another friend of ours, Midge. She lived in Burnham-on-Sea, which was not too far from my home. We used to meet whenever we could on a Friday evening and one of the group would always open up by saying a prayer, prayers are so important, it does not cost us anything to say a prayer but it means so much, no matter how short they are.

We had asked for healing, protection and guidance for each and everyone of us whilst we were there that night, as well as help and that everything would be done in truth, love and light. When the prayer had finished I would talk the group into a meditation which would usually consist of a walk to a certain point somewhere, I would then leave the group at that point for about ten to fifteen minutes and then I would walk them back to the beginning, all the group would then talk and discuss what they had experienced on this journey. The idea of a meditation is to help a person to go within themselves, to see whether they had seen anybody or whether they had felt anything, or if they had generally felt more aware. You find that when someone has a meditation exercise it calms them down, they begin to feel relaxed and more at ease, I find this definitely helps people that lack confidence.

Before closing the evening, we would send out healing to all those in our healing books (as each one of us has our own healing book, with many names in it), there are no limits to the amount of names you can put in these books. We would then send healing to all the areas around the world that needed healing that night and the planet earth. By doing this we would use all the energy that had been built in the circle to help others.

I was still attending the Blue Cross Circle on a Monday night whenever possible, although I was beginning to feel that I had to discontinue this soon in order to help my own development. But as it so happened, the open circle was finishing that night for a six week break.

The open circle would consist of up to 20 people of which one person would be in charge, there would be prayers said at the beginning, and then we would be given a small meditation after which we would 'give off' whatever we had picked up during that period and try to link into other people within the circle as well, it would then close with a prayer. This would take approximately an hour and a half in total.

On December 29th Shileen visited my group. She gave them a small mediation at the beginning in order that we may tune in with one thing in particular that suited each one of us, we then had an exercise which consisted of eight different types of book. Each one was placed in a brown envelope so that no-one (including Shileen) knew what kind of book was where. Each one of the group picked out an envlope and then Shileen asked us all to sense the title of the book or what it was about. After we had all voiced our opinions we were allowed to take the book out of the envelope to see if we were on the right track or not, some of us were. Shileen then asked us to open the book at random and to choose a short paragraph to read and we were amazed, because the meditation, the book and the paragraph were all linked together and yet there were various types of books (as I have previously said) antique books, healing books, books of mediumship, all kinds of books but each one was relevant to each person in its own way.

Shileen has so much talent, both as a Medium and as a Teacher but she lacks confidence within herself, as I find so many good Mediums do.

Again when the evening had finished we used the energy that had been built up by sending it out for healing.

Not long afterwards I was given a book called 'The Quiet Mind', sayings of White Eagle. A work colleague of mine, Ken

Clark, who is very interested in spiritualism, gave it to me and explained that if I had a particular question that I would like answered, just to open the book at random and read the paragraph that I am drawn to and my question would be answered.

I find this little book very useful and comforting, and I would recommend any of you to get one and try it.

On the last day of December 1989, Shileen and I went to the Blue Cross Church, and our friend Lil, took the chair for the first time, she chaired the service like a true professional putting so much love, thought and truth into the service, that the people in the congregation were awakened by the love that was flowing from her. I really felt for her that day because normally she lacks confidence in herself but here she was chairing for the first time with a wonderful compassion as if she had been chairing for years.

I noticed Lil was wearing the Canterbury Cross I had given to her some months previously and she told me afterwards that she had received so much help and healing when she wore this cross, she related to me an experience that one night as she and her husband lay in bed the temperature in the room became quite unbearable, it was the cross which had caused the heat as it was giving out healing to both of them, but Lil felt that she needed to remove the cross from the bedroom, this she did and immediately the room returned to normal temperature.

This made me realise just what was in this cross I had given to her, as it was given with love for healing and help.

The following month I travelled back to Basildon with Shileen. She took me to meet two friends of hers, Betty and Ian, who were both Psychics, they gave me a message that night and part of it was from Phillip, he explained something to me that I needed to know, Shileen then shocked me, by asking me to give Betty and Ian a reading myself, this was something I did not think I was capable of as I too, lacked confidence, because I was just learning and we will always learn, as long as we live.

Here you can see from the times and dates in this book how

things happen to me; sometimes quickly and other times slowly because one of the biggest things we all must learn is patience. This is why I am trying to show you how my gradual progression and learning has helped me and I am hoping it will help you, as I received so much help from my friends in spirit, by learning to communicate with them.

I gave Betty and Ian a reading that night which they both accepted and were very pleased with, much to my surprise.

Again, on the Thursday, Shileen introduced me to another of her friends and asked me also to give this friend a reading but this time using a crystal ball, Shileen's friend could relate to everything I had given her. This made me feel really good and amazed, I thanked my helpers that had been with me for giving me the information that they had done, that was needed that night.

On Friday 5th January 1990, I gave my first talk and demonstration on healing, this took place at the Pyramid of Friends in Basildon and I know in myself that it went really well. I was very pleased with the way that everyone reacted who attended. There was approximately 36 people in total and I started the evening by explaining to everyone how I had come into the movement and into healing, this was the reason Phillip had come to me on that Wednesday night at Betty and Ian's house, as I needed to know how I should start.

Again many people received healing that night and I collected 46 names for my absent healing book. I gave out my cards but I did not explain to everyone how to use them as for some reason I was being very cautious. When the evening had finished there were tears of joy streaming down the faces of several of the congregation and the lady who had organised the evening asked what everybody had thought, they all replied that they thought the talk and demonstration had been done with the true emotions of love and they were all left with a really good feeling as they made their way home.

Amongst the many people I met that night was a lady called Brenda, she contacted me on the Saturday morning and asked me if I could go with her to visit her mother in hospital (her mother had had a stroke previously and been admitted in an unconscious state and was very ill). The family felt she was ready to pass over into spirit, they asked me if I could give their mother healing and give them any advice. When I got into the mother's room she was lying there in bed, and was surrounded by her two sons and two daughters, I could feel from her mother that she was putting up a terrific fight.

At certain times in our life we have to realise that we are going to pass over, and yes, we do think of the individuals we are going to leave behind – how are they going to cope? I talked to that lady, even though she was unconcious (we must realise that an unconcious person retains their awareness even though they can't respond, we all tend to underestimate an unconcious person). I asked the lady to rest and also asked her spirit friends to help her, I asked the family the same and to let her find peace and let God take over as she needed to rest – even though I knew it would be difficult for them to let her go, but we have to love someone enough to have the strength to say goodbye.

The day afterwards she passed away peacefully.

CHAPTER SIX

A RED ROSE

On Monday the 8th December I called at my local news-agents to collect a copy of the Psychic News. This is a weekly paper and contains many interesting and varied psychic and spiritual stories, and a friend said,

'I have just written to them'.

I thought he meant the Psychic News but talking further I realised that he had written to the Harry Edward's Healing Sanctuary. He told me that his six-year-old son was suffering from cancer and I explained to him how I intended to dedicate my life to healing and that I would send his son healing thoughts.

I invited him to bring his son to my home but he did not wish to do this as he did not want to alarm the young boy in any way. Instead he gave me a photograph of his son and his name and I placed both these in my healing book. I asked that he would receive all the help and healing he needed, also not forgetting his family.

Later that day I was at my home, reading the Psychic News, and I felt myself drawn to an article on the Harry Edwards Healing Sanctuary, I started to pick up my confirmation signal that Harry Edwards was responding to a call for help for that young boy. This made me pleased to know that such a dedicated man was responding to my call for help.

On Wednesday 10th December, some friends came round and we talked and discussed various aspects of spiritual work. We gave one another healing, and again I experienced a spirit hand on my shoulder whilst I was receiving healing. If you ever experience anything like this, I don't think you will ever forget it, it's such a wonderful feeling.

At this time I joined the World Federation of Healing who would give me help over the years to come. The World Federation of Healing was initiated in 1975 at Westfield College, London University. From the 14 countries represented at the conference in 1975, it has slowly grown to include membership in more than 30 countries.

It is unique organisation because it's aims are to unite all practitioners in the healing fields, whether they be doctors of Allopathic or Homeopathic persuasion, alternative therapists, ministers of religion healers etc. The World Federation of Healing now includes in its membership practitioners in more than 50 different therapies.

An indication of the wide interest in this organisation is that of the seven presidents, three have been medical doctors.

The World Federation of Healing was one of the founder members of the confederation of healing organisations (CHO) which is the national organisation that officially represents the main healing organisations in the United Kingdom. If you would like to know more about its history, aims and objectives or how to join then write, enclosing an s.a.e, to:

Membership Secretary
Mrs Doris Jones
10 The Close
Addington Park
Nr Maidstone
Kent
England
ME19 5BL

I still continued to visit Churches and demonstrations whenever and wherever possible, and whilst I was in Essex I managed to visit four different kinds of Spiritualist Churches. I was really pleased with the way I felt as each one 'gave off' its own independent feelings of love, of the hard work that was going on in these Churches, how they were trying to reach people and how genuine the people were attending them.

On the 19th January, I travelled to Dukinfield again to visit my parents, whilst there I attended a talk on science and spiritualism at Hyde Church. This was given by a Professor from Bath. He gave this talk from a scientist's point of view. It was very different to what I was used to hearing and several of the people attending did not like it. But I feel that we have to look at all aspects of spiritualism and if we come across something like this where we don't agree with what is being said, I recommend that we try and reverse roles with that person to put ourselves in their position and to look at why they are thinking in the way they do, then come back to ourself. Now sometimes we still don't agree with them after, but what a great way to find out if we are right by changing roles and thinking like they do for that particular time. This gives us a far wider outlook as we must always be prepared to question everything and everyone to ensure that what we get in the end is love, light and truth, it's not less holy to question. We should never be afraid to question our guides and helpers, remembering that they too are learning each day with us, and each question we ask helps their development, never be scared of questioning them because they've passed.

I met a young woman at this demonstration called Anthea, we talked about our mutual interest in spiritualism and she said she would be taking a course in Bristol connected with her work, so I arranged to meet her when she came down in order that we may continue our discussions.

On the 1st February 1990 I gave my second talk and demonstration on healing. Shileen again, had arranged it. This time it was to take place in Hornchurch, approximately 30 people attended that night and again I collected more names for my absent healing book. What we must realise is that it is not just up to an individual to help people, we must look at ourselves as being part of a team as a team can help reach so many more people, a team consists of not only people from the earth plane but spirit helpers as well, so many people have gifts of their own that are spiritual and if all these people get together and send out help, it would be so much stronger. I want you to recognise that.

Whilst I was giving healing to a man that night at the demonstration, Shileen could see spiritually he had a growth inside his stomach, even though he was receiving orthodox treatment for it, the growth that night was removed by the healing and the man had to excuse himself in order to go and be sick, to clear it out of his system.

Healing does this sometimes, the body will react by removing anything that is not needed within our system, there can never be any guarantee with healing that you will be cured, never any guarantee at all that it will actually work. Many times healing takes place over a period of time before any benefit is felt. We must always look to healing being a complementary way to work alongside other methods of medicines, not an alternative method. Some people may react to healing up to 24 hours later in order to remove the illness, it is the body's way of dealing with the problem, sometimes they may have something like bruises which come out of their skin even though there has been no hard treatment, no rough hands, there is never any need for manipulation in healing this is just the bodies reaction where the body is rejecting the illness.

I bumped into an old friend whilst I was in Essex, Marie Wakeling (who I met at Hayling Island) we had a lot to talk about and discuss. It was nice to be able to talk to her after not seeing her for so long, and we both learnt a lot from each other.

I find that as I go around meeting and talking to Mediums and Healers or people who are just genuinely interested in spiritualism, a large amount of learning can be done by collecting and storing information given from other people, for us to use whenever we can. We can learn a vast amount from each other, spirit also learns by watching and listening to us. When someone passes to the world of spirit they don't suddenly know everything at once. They too, have to learn, just like we do here, on the earth plane and we can learn together as this is the road so important to recognise, it is vital that we learn and work together as a team, not just as one individual or one spirit. So often I find ego moves in to certain people and actually blocks them from learning and affects the way they work which is a shame.

Dot Matthews managed to come to my home again in February, and so I invited some friends around to join us in a circle. It is just wonderful to see how Dot works, how her guides talk through her and how she helps so many people (all this time I was still recording my messages and writing them up in my books. I now had a collection of over 70 tapes).

My friend Midge was beginning to show signs of an illness. I discovered she had cancer so I began giving Midge touch healing whenever I had the opportunity and sent her absent healing every day.

Early in February Midge and I got the opportunity to visit Exeter Cathedral, it was there that we discovered on the ceiling a roof boss that had been painted of Thomas Beckett and I felt that this was the reason we had been drawn to go there.

I ask you to try and understand that we all need to work on our development, some of us are not lucky enough to receive the gift from spirit immediately or to recognise it. We have to work at it and even when we receive it do we fully understand and appreciate it? I ask myself, and I ask you also, to look at this, would we appreciate our gifts if they were given to us "on a plate?"

My group was still meeting regularly on a Friday night, one night I let the group do psychometry. This involves giving a personal item, eg ring, watch etc. This person then holds the item and proceeds to give a message to its owner by 'picking up' off the item. The group did very well that night and I was pleased.

On the 27th February, as I was sat at home I began picking up Doris Stokes, a red rose, Marie Wakeling and Laingdon Church, although I did not know why.

On the 1st March, I travelled to Basildon to visit Shileen and to attend a talk on numerology. As the name suggests, it involves numbers. Numerologists use a table of numbers, each number having a specific meaning, then clients can have a reading by giving their date of birth to a Numerologist who in turn equates this to a number in a table and therefore gives a reading from it. I was not over-impressed by this at all but again, numerology is another aspect which we must look at. Some people can be helped by numerology and there are some very good people who work with it, because this method of working suits them.

On the Saturday afternoon, I made my way to see Marie and explained to her what I had picked up in February, she informed me that she had been very good friends with Doris Stokes and that she will always think of her with a red rose. When Doris had passed to the world of spirit and she was lying in the Chapel of Rest, Marie went to buy her a red rose to put in her hand, but when she got to the florist there were no red roses available. Marie was then going to buy some freesias but a spirit voice said to her 'no', she found out afterwards when she arrived at the Chapel there were freesias everywhere even so she still remembers Doris with a red rose.

I asked her,

'why "Laingdon Church"? '

'you have to work there one day', she told me.

That same day I happened to visit Laingdon Church but I did not mention to anyone the message that I had received, as the evening was drawing to a close I was approached and asked if I would be willing to do a talk and demonstration on healing, this was another way of giving confirmation really.

One of the ladies who also attended my first talk at the Pyramid of Friends was also there, after I had given the talk at the Pyramid I sent her a copy of the book which I previously told you about – The Quiet Mind – and she proceeded to tell me that she had been given a message at a Spiritualist Church telling her that someone would be sending her a book and they had explained to her how to use it, this is yet another way of how spirit works.

I also took up the advantage of attending a Psychic Supper at the Pyramid whilst I was in Essex (for those of you who have never attended one of these, it involves groups of people sitting at tables, a Medium then sits at each one of these tables and proceeds to give readings to the people sat at their table). If you can visualise several of these tables, each with a Medium trying to give a reading to all the other people sat at the table, very close together in a small room, and whilst all this is going on supper was being served, even though the people were supposed to wait until the Medium had finished giving the readings, unfortunately not everyone did, so this created what was obviously a very difficult atmosphere to work in. Very psychic and not at all spiritual, as the right vibrations were not there, this was the first one I had ever attended and I was not impressed.

Myself doing a talk and demonstration

On the Sunday night Shileen and I visited a Spiritualist Church that had not been open very long in a place called Leigh although this Church was new it had a lovely feeling within it. There were several people attending the service and I received a message again from the Medium and later went on to discover that the Church was in use virtually every day of the week for healing, demonstrations, services, discussions and prayers, also 'questions answered' sessions. Each day, or part of the day the Church was in use. This is very unusual to see nowadays, but it is very good if you can manage it as it allows you to reach more people, and create a better atmosphere within the Church.

The following Thursday, Anthea rang me and informed me that she too had received a message in Church from a Medium, the previous Saturday. She was told about the two of us meeting and how she travelled down to my part of the country and the Medium had known that Anthea had a very special gift of her own with regards to healing. Anthea works with handicapped children, the type of work she does and the way she carries it out is a way of healing in its own right, like I have explained before, healing comes in many different forms and ways, you do not always have to touch the person who requires healing, we need to use love and be caring.

I told Anthea, whilst we were on the phone, that she would be asked to go to America for a time to tell others about her work with the mentally handicapped children.

On the 16th March, Midge and myself made our way to Porlock, just outside of which, we discovered a very small Church in the valleys. Here we saw a monument in memory of the author who wrote Lorna Doone (if you are ever in this area I would recommend you visit this small church). It is such a beautiful church, just an ordinary country one, but so beautiful within itself and what a lovely spot it is situated in.

On the 21st March a friend of mine from Blue Cross and myself travelled to Belgrave Square in London, which is the Spiritualist Association Headquarters, thousands of people each year visit there; some for healing, some for readings or demonstrations and others just to look around the building itself. Personally I was disgusted with the state of the building, everywhere looked dirty to me and I felt there was not an ounce of love within that building, in my opinion the vibrations were just not right at all when I attended that day. The real flowers had long past their best and needed throwing away, and the dried flowers were covered in dust, I was so disappointed with the feeling that I picked up from this building, especially when I thought about all the people who attended there each year expecting love and healing, and after all this place is supposed to reflect the spiritualist movement, imagine what people must think if they saw the place like I did.

I watched a demonstration in the afternoon by a lady Medium called Coral Puldge. She is better known as a Psychic Artist. This particular afternoon she was giving a demonstration of clairvoyance, whilst she was proceeding with her demonstration giving a message to a young lady in the audience, an electric fire exploded (the fire was plugged in although it was not switched on), but the Medium continued talking, unaffected, to give the message to this young lady, whose husband (I discovered later on) had been killed in an explosion in Ireland. Here was a true professional working which I admired.

NOTES AND FEELINGS

CHAPTER SEVEN

PIPE OF PEACE

People often ask, "what happens to us when we die?" Nearly everyone is afraid of dying. This is the time when we come to meet our friends that have passed before us, they wait for us and greet us as we come to leave our physical body and go to the spirit world. People always talk about heaven and hell, to me hell is where we are today on the earth plane, heaven is the spirit world but it's not up in the sky like everyone thinks, it's all around us in several dimensions. Our friends meet us and take us to the spirit world and if we've been suffering with pain we go through a rehabilitation period where we are helped in spirit hospitals to recognise that we no longer have that pain, that suffering, that trauma which we had whilst in our earthly bodies, often when we make contact with our friends on the earth plane we make the Medium aware of the pain we actually suffered so that then the person that we are communicating with recognises who we are. People who have lost limbs here on earth regain them in their spiritual body, but they would return to us without them so we can recognise who they are. This is just a demonstration to us, for our benefit, as they do have everything they have lost, returned.

In the spirit world the colours and the lights are far more vivid and brilliant than here on the earth plane, the flowers, the animals, again are far, far superior to what we see here on the earth plane. We still keep all our memories of the earth plane. Often people say why hasn't their loved ones contacted them when may be they've been passed for a few years? I believe this is due to them not recognising how long they have been gone, as time for spirit is not relevant.

Sometimes our friends when they pass don't recognise that they have done so, they would still join us in our meetings and gatherings, but unfortunately cannot understand why we don't acknowledge what they are saying to us, this is simply because we are not capable of picking them up from the level they are on and communicating with them. I hope this simple explanation answers some of your questions. Sometimes spirit remain earth bound because they miss that link which takes them to the spirit world for whatever reason. Quite often, we ourselves can hold them back with the love we have for them because basically we are saying to ourselves,

'don't go, please don't go',

so they miss that link and will need help at another time to make that journey complete, quite often this is where groups or individuals come in to their own being with a gift they have been granted, to help spirits that are earth bound.

My group was still meeting and on the 23rd March, we had a flower sensitive evening, where each one of us took a flower of our choice, which only we had come in contact with, we all placed the flowers on the table, making sure they didn't touch, then each of us picked a flower of our choice, not choosing our own, then proceeded to give a reading from it without knowing whose flower it was. This was rather interesting and very successful but I recommend that if you do take a flower for a flower sensitive reading, try not to take one with thorns on the stem for obvious reasons.

About this time, I attended a seminar on crystals, I was surprised to learn of the apparent energy and power contained in a crystal. Again, if you have the opportunity to come in contact with anyone associated with crystals I would recommend that you talk to them as it is something different and you might learn something useful for yourself, like having a particular feeling about a certain type of crystal or size that you are drawn to. Crystals give off a vibration of their own, people can use these for good or bad purposes, in some cases we are not aware of a power contained in a crystal, let alone have the ability to control it, I ask you to make your own mind up about crystals but be aware of their strengths.

On the 26th March, I attended the open circle again at Blue Cross. This time, during my meditation, I was met by an Indian on a white horse and he told me that I would need all my strength, courage, cunning and wisdom for what I had to do. He took me into a cave and showed me some very old Indian Tombs he then allowed me to sit down and talk to him and the other Indians that were present, they were all very old and wise, I learnt a lot from what they had to say and appreciated the knowledge they gave me.

After this I 'saw' a small metal cross with one of the women who were in the circle that night, I saw this spiritually and when the circle was finished I told her about it, she told me that she had lost this cross three weeks previously and it had completely vanished, but later that night she rang me at home to say it had returned, it was just lying on the window sill in her bedroom when she got home, this lady lives on her own and there was no way anyone else could have removed it and put it back, except spirit.

Spirit can and will, make items appear and disappear or even move them to make you more aware of their presence and power. This should not be confused with poltergiest actions, as they are a whole different ball game altogether.

The following night Anthea rang me again to tell me that she had been asked to go to America to work, this confirmed what I had told her a few weeks previously.

At the end of March, Dot Matthews came down to stay with me again for the week (as she was serving the Blue Cross Church for that weekend). After the Sunday evening service had finished Dot told me that she felt someone had just passed into the world of spirit with a tumour, even though I did not know who it was at that time I still accepted it, I didn't find out until the following day that this person who had passed was my ex-mother-in-law, Gladys.

The following night Dot and myself attended the Blue Cross Open Circle and again, I was aware of another Indian with me during my meditation. An Indian guide who called himself Grey Wolf came and talked through Dot whilst she was in trance, he proceeded to talk to the circle and also offered the pipe of peace for everyone to smoke with him. He explained how he had spent a long time on the mountain before he had actually died, and told us how he watched over all of us which gave everyone in the circle something to think about that night.

On the 4th April, I took Dot to Glastonbury Abbey and whilst there we went into a small Chapel situated on the Abbey site. Dot started working and picking up various spirit helpers and messages which I had the opportunity of recording, to see Dot working this way is an experience which unfortunately many of us will not witness during our lifetime, as we just don't seem to have the time or the dedication to learn like she did. Dot learnt the old fashioned way of becoming a Medium, where you may just sit each week for up to 2 years for one or two evenings in a chair, upright, and do breathing exercises. Of course, there was no televisions then, our way of life has changed and I think our methods of learning must also change and we must adapt to them, by me saying adapt with the times, I do not mean that we will turn out to be Mediums overnight, it does take time and patience, but most of all dedication. Dedication means getting to your group meeting or demonstration early – not just turning up exactly on time, don't even bother if you're going to be late. Dedication means going in all weathers – even when you're tired. Think about it before you commit yourself please.

On Saturday 7th April, Dot and myself travelled to Pontypridd in Wales where Dot was to conduct yet another demonstration of her Mediumship. This gave me my first opportunity to chair for a demonstration, it lasted approximately 3 hours as we had no time restrictions and was held in a small village hall with about 30 people attending. I learnt so much from that day, on how to help and control a situation like a demonstration. I felt proud to be able to chair for Dot because she was such a marvellous worker. Dot and myself were looked after well in Pontypridd, which I felt helped Dot's performance.

Do we look after our Mediums when they conduct our services and demonstrations for us? Often they travel long distances without food or refreshments, Do we provide these when they come to our Church? Do we find them a suitable room to rest in and refresh themselves before conducting a service? Often we don't, we fail in our responsibilities to assist our brothers and sisters that are committing their lives to working for spirit by demonstrating their gift to us. Everyone needs that comfort, that food, the liquid refreshments every day, but often after a journey of may be 3 or 4 hours there is not even anybody to meet them at the Church door when they arrive early which should always be the case. The committee members may turn up some 10 minutes before the service is due to start and there is nothing for our Medium. Look at this if you have any responsibilities within your Churches to bettering the conditions for the Mediums that serve our Churches today, it's important that they are looked after and treated properly.

On the 9th of April, I travelled to London where another friend of mine Elaine lives, and we went around Westminster Abbey together. I found that whilst walking around, my spiritual feelings were so strong, I had never ever felt them this strong within any of the Churches or Abbeys I had visited, I felt that this was due to the amount of spirits that are in Westminster Abbey. Since then I have returned to Westminster three times and as yet have not felt spirit as strong.

On the 21st April, I attended Summer School, again at Torbay. That week I watched Mavis Pittilla, Eric Hatton and Gordon Higginson give talks and demonstrations on various aspects connected with spiritualism and spiritual work.

I also had a psychic drawing done by a man called Nan Crook, this was of a Buddhist Monk who Nan said was with me at that particular time, the illustration turned out to be quite good.When I look at this picture in my home I often see a younger Monk stood in the corner where it is hanging.

On the Thursday, Gordon Higginson gave a talk on his definition of how we should see the changes within spiritualism and how there should be something done to improve the standards of Mediumship and Healers who give demonstrations. So I asked him a question regarding what he would do to put these matters right, unfortunately he did not answer me direct, and passed it on to his panel whom I felt all made different excuses, why it was not being done right and why it was not being run correctly. My own personal views are that people should be doing something about the standards but they don't seem to be motivated enough to put their money where their mouth is!

I remember meeting Gordon Higginson once before at Hyde Church. After he had done an evening demonstration to a packed audience, I asked if I could see him for a moment or two, to ask his advice. I was shown into a small room where Gordon was resting but he made me welcome and I asked him if he could help me as I wanted to devote my life to healing. His words to me were:

'Forget it, unless you have another profession like being a Reflexologist, Hypnotist, Accupuncturist etc'.

I could not believe what he was saying to me! I thanked him for his time but made my mind up that I would not 'forget it', I was now even more determined to become a Healer.

When I returned home on the Saturday, I attended a Spiritualist Church at Bridgwater where the chairman gave me a small message afterwards, he told me that he could see a Buddhist Monk with me. This was yet another confirmation for me of what I had been given in my drawing by Nan Crook. I always look for that extra confirmation, and think it is important that you do too.

On the 29th April 1990, I attended a Spiritualist Church that was new to me, situated at Frenchay in Bristol. It had originally been a barn and now it had been converted into a lovely Spiritualist Church, quite large in size and very brightly painted (it was situated in the grounds of a home for handicapped children). You were greeted very pleasantly as you sat down, the chairperson, Jim Edbrook would come and shake hands with every individual to make you feel welcome, and you did with that lovely feeling which came from the Church and flowed outside.

Frenchay Church, the Manor House (where Aunt Eida lives) and their grounds have a wonderful story behind them;

In 1941 a young 26-year-old lady Eida Tidder, an active Baptist, was training to become a nurse to go into the mission field. During this time she took ill with a kidney complaint, so she decided to move to Bristol from London so her parents couldn't see her suffering. When she was in Bristol for an interview she befriended a lady who offered to let her stay with her as she lived on her own as her husband was away in the war, so Eida moved into her home but she was not happy. In the same cul-de-sac lived Olive and Arthur Clark with their two children in a small two bedroom bungalow. Olive used to collect for different organisations around the houses, and soon her and Eida became good friends, when one day, Olive Burnt her arm badly. So Eida looked after her with the skills she had learnt by training to be a nurse, enabling Olive to stay at home with her children.

In time Eida's health was deteriorating and she began seeing her doctor three or four times a week, X-rays showed how bad her kidneys were.

Before long Eida was taken seriously ill so Olive went to stay with her, to help her with her ailment, eventually she suggested that Eida should move to live with her and her family although room in the bungalow was limited.

Eida accepted and moved into their living room. Both Olive and Arthur were strong spiritualists and asked if Eida would receive healing. To keep the peace Eida said 'Yes' and in no time at all she began to get better.

Eida became a health visitor working in the poor areas of Bristol, often she would bring the affected children home to stop with the Clarks.

Arthur suggested that they look for somewhere bigger to cater for all of them.

One day whilst driving a friend about who happened to be an MP, Mr. J. H. Alpass, she related her wishes when suddenly he told her to turn into a driveway up to a large manor house whereupon he took Eida to the door and after they entered negotiated a lease for five years.

Eida had also returned to the doctors for an X-ray and to their surprise they found no trace of her kidney complaint. It had vanished completely.

Olive and Arthur sold their bungalow and with the £1,000 left over moved in to the manor house. There were so many youngsters requiring help everyone worked long hours to help, and Arthur still had his full time job. When he came home at night he wasn't able to stop. He had to make up feeds for the babies. Many of their spiritualist friends helped them but it was still hard work.

Whenever a job had to be done the builders would be called in. Then the bills arrived Eida and Olive would ask spirit to help and each time they received the exact amount of money they needed, in the form of collections etc.

All kinds of children have benefited from their home.

In the beginning they were told they would have a church in their grounds but this did not happen until the roof of the barn caved in one day. This was then eventually converted into the Church as it is today.

The Clarks have passed away but Auntie Eida is still living strong at the fine age of 77-years-old.

So many people have received help from the work of these three people.

I would like to thank them for all their good work.

CHAPTER EIGHT

FRANCE

On the 3rd May, I travelled to Essex to give a talk and demonstration. I did feel that I could have done better that night, although what did disappoint me was the people who had invited me there continually attacked everything I said, and tried to bring up many other subjects which were not relevant with healing, and which their own views were very strong on. They were basically trying to put their point of view across that night and I felt they were trying to brainwash the other members of the Church into their own way of thinking, which you should never try to do. We must always have our own point of view and always go along with our own feelings, immaterial of who tells us what, where or when.

On the 5th April, I attended a Red Indian Exhibition with Shileen in London. Whilst there I managed to purchase three large prints and various cards depicting Indians and their way of life. I managed to get these prints framed and they now hang in my home and Sanctuary. These, I feel, are rather significant to me and I get so much from them when I look and read the words on the prints.

On the 13th May, whilst attending the service at a local Spiritiualist Church, I began to feel ill, I felt that someone was draining me, eventually I picked out the man in question whom

I found out afterwards came with the Medium. I felt that he was taking other peoples energies to give the Medium strength on the platform. I do not believe that this was done in a correct and safe way let alone ethical, and to me the people running the Church did not even know what was going on, which is one of the responsibilities of a chair-person, I hope this shows you how easily we can be drained.

I strongly believe that many of the people who chair at demonstrations or services don't recognise the many areas they are responsible for, quite often I've seen chairpersons looking grubby, untidy, half asleep and just not aware of what is going on around them. They should at least wash and dress accordingly for the part!

Do they present themselves correctly? Can everyone hear, see and understand them? Do they know the format of the demonstration or service fully themselves? (I think many have lost touch with spiritualism nowadays) do they explain fully what it is all about and what you can do to help the demonstator? Are all the lights on before it goes dark so they are not turned on half-way through the service disturbing the speaker and audience? Are the doors open or closed as they should be? What about the emergency exits - are they clear and unlocked? Can they cope with whatever problems may arise whilst they are chairing? For example: power cuts, the Medium feeling unwell, the Medium having difficulty whilst working, the clock stopping, people in the congregation making a scene against spiritualism, is everything managed and organised before the start? Many people can become a good chairperson if given the chance and training. Please, next time you watch a service look at the chairperson with these points in mind, how would you improve on their performance?

On the 14th May, I travelled to Belgrave Square in London again. Here I met my first overseas contact, a girl called Sara from Israel, we seemed to meet accidentally for just a few moments of our time, in the canteen area at Belgrave Square and I realised almost immediately that Sara was capable of many spiritual things and I told her so. She informed me that in Israel they do not talk about such things, she had travelled to England to take a course which had been cancelled, it was a healing and counselling course that she had come for. So she had made her way to Belgrave Square to have a look around. Sara then asked me out of the blue for one of my cards which meant to me that one of her spirit helpers was telling her about my card. I know that one day we shall meet again but I don't know where or when.

Sara runs two Healing Sanctuaries in Israel and she was also trying to get enough money together in England to open a third one, I do look forward to that day when I meet her again.

About the same time, I was asked to do a service at Wells Spiritualist Church on the 27th May, I had never done a service before and I was really looking forward to it but unfortunately when the day arrived the service was cancelled due to some other event taking place in the building they were using. I believe this was spirit's way of telling me I'm not ready to take a service here.

On the 3rd June 1990, I travelled to Dukinfield to stay with my parents again, and on the Monday I travelled to York with my friend, Anthea, as we were to visit the Spiritualist Church which I had been to the year before, and who should I meet in there but the same lady that had led me from the derelict Church all that time ago. We watched a talk and demonstration that afternoon and afterwards I took the opportunity of talking to this lady and discovered her name was Madge and she lived in the village of Pocklington (not far away from Beverley Minster) Madge proceeded to tell me about that day we first met, that she had been told by spirit to go around to the old Church to meet me and then guide me to the new Church.

She asked me if I would give her healing which I did and I picked up that she was suffering from Multiple Sclerosis. It was not until we were on the train coming home that I remembered the message I had been given that day in Gloucester by June that I would visit York again and that I would go on the train. I had never given it a thought when I got on the train but here I was, I should not have doubted what spirit have given me, question it - yes, but not doubt it.

On Thursday of that week, Anthea and I travelled up to Derbyshire. While we were in a small village (called Eyam), we came across a little church called St Lawrences, as we were walking around the grave yard, I became aware of spirit telling me that Anthea had lived here in this village in a previous life, a few hundred years before (there had been a plague in Eyam where over 200 people had died). When we went inside the Church, on display was a book with all the names of those who had died in the plague, I pointed out to Anthea the names of two people within the Register that I was being told she had been one of them. Anthea, before, had had some form of confirmation whilst she was in the church yard to tell her there was something very strong there that she should know about, we both wondered whether this was a co-incidence or what, as we had actually found this church yard by accident and that we had all these feelings and emotions whilst we were there.

During the next few months, although she lives in Hyde, Anthea had this village confirmation 'given' to her in various ways, shapes and forms, it was mentioned to her in conversations at work, there was a play put on at school all about the village plague and somewhere else she visited stemmed originally from this small village.

Spirit messages are sometimes just little bits of evidence and co-incidences that set our own bells ringing, which we need then to work on and follow through, or we can choose to ignore it if we wish, it is in the end up to us.

On the Friday night I gave a demonstration and talk in Hyde Church, approximately 40 people attended and I thought it went very well, there were many questions asked from the people there. I also got them to take part in the demonstration by both giving and receiving healing, then seeing what they felt, following this I was invited back (which is always a good sign). Whilst there I obtained more names for my healing book, I do think it is important that whatever you are teaching you do come across in the correct way. That you always look smart in your appearance, and always maintain complete control of the group which you are teaching or talking to, you should allow them the freedom of questions right from the beginning, as it is so much easier but discipline is important, especially whilst teaching, after all Teachers are role-models for their students.

I put the names that I had been given in my healing book. There is no limit to the number of people or animals, we wish to place in our healing books. Spirit will always reach them.

On the Saturday night I went to Denton Church again, where I received a message from the lady Medium that night, I also met another lady there, who invited me back to her house on the Sunday to give me a tea leaf reading - a tea reading is definitely different; first of all you need to drink the tea, after I had drunk it the lady turned my cup around three times and then turned it upside down, once she had done this she looked into the cup and proceeded to give me a reading.

There was several things in this reading which I could accept although I felt she worked more on a psychic level than spiritual, again people use, at times, materialistic things to help them give readings, I don't object to them, I always say they should go along with how they feel and with what works best for them.

My group tried tea-leaf reading but it proved rather un-successful, I just put it down to each individual and how they felt, everybody has their own preference but it is good to explore new fields, provided you have got the right supervision in controlling the group, as discipline and protection, of course, are so important.

On the 28th June I started another one of my journeys, this time it was different, we travelled to France to make our way to a large farmhouse owned by my ex-wife Beryl, the farm dated back to about the 16th century and is situated about 5 miles away from the nearest village, the driveway itself leading to the farm takes some time to get up as it is over a mile long! The

Farmhouse in France

farmhouse's main building was over 130 feet in length and there was very little furniture in the building so it was virtually bare. As I entered the house I was pleasantly surprised as I saw a spirit lady busy working in one of the rooms, this created an air of happiness immediately, but only I saw it.

With me for a few days was my son, Steven, and two of his friends, my ex-wife Beryl and her husband Pete. On the first night we slept there I became aware of the house coming alive with spirit people walking around. What I did not realise was the others had not slept there before as they had used a caravan whilst the house needed doing up, all the accommodation was situated downstairs with various bedrooms and bathrooms etc, and the upstairs part of the house was an empty barn with a quarry tiled floor which stretched the full length of the house. This was obviously used by the farmer for keeping his hay to feed his animals throughout the winter, which also kept the heat in the house I suppose.

On the Friday night just after we had all gone to bed and the lights were switched off, my son Steven let out a scream, I thought he was just playing about with his mates (as we were all sharing the same room), but I discovered the following day that he had felt a spirit hand touch his head and brush back his hair. Mentally I asked spirit why had they done this and I became aware of them telling me that they had just done it because they had wanted to look at Steven, just to see what makes him tick and see how he would respond.

The house was full of many spirit people I felt and even though at night it became alive with them, this did not worry me. Beryl, became aware of them throughout the day and she was not amused, I can assure you. As she too, had heard the noises of the spirit people walking around and on the Saturday night, whilst Steven, one of his friends and me were outside, Steven discovered that he could see spirit, he saw members of the French Resistance around a table drinking, enjoying the life they used to when on the earth plane, sure enough as the night approached the noises again, started throughout the house.

On the Sunday, I was left on my own (as everyone else was travelling on to Spain). So during the following week I proceeded to work on this book and becoming more and more aware of spirit activity myself. I could sense more and feel more when they were around. I would get my confirmation signal and I began seeing soldiers from the second world war, walking down the drive. These were German soldiers. At first I put it down to my imagination. I couldn't definitely say yes at that time.

On the Wednesday morning, whilst travelling through one of the local villages, I happened to phone my friend Midge, for no reason (except she was on my mind). She was out at the time but I left a message on her answering machine and she rang me back later that night, when she told me that she had to go into Bristol Royal Infirmary to receive treatment for cancer. The hospital had said that she had cancer near her brain, she was in a lot of pain and things did not look too good for her at all.

One afternoon, whilst walking around the farmhouse, I went into an area where the steps were to climb into the attic. As I did so my hair stood on end (what little I have got!) I was aware of very strong spirit activity around me but it did not frighten me, although I was a little nervous, I decided to walk up the stairs into the attic, I then proceeded to walk the full length of the attic in order that I might find out what it was that I was picking up.

I managed to open a window at the far end of the attic and also an outer door, half way along (that was when I discovered that the attic was 130 metres long, as I counted every single step I made). About half way back I became aware that in a certain spot I could spiritually see some French Jews hiding in a corner, with fear, these were earthbound spirits that had remained at the farmhouse since the last war. The reason I had seen the German Soldiers was now obvious to me. They had been coming to find the Jews that were hiding on the farm. I communicated with these spirits, mentally and that night I said a prayer for these spirit friends, asking that they may be released from this point and taken away to be helped as there was no longer any need for them to remain.

Again, on the Thursday night, I said another prayer. The spirit activity was very intense that night, in which an old Frenchman played a part. He was trying to tell me something, although he talked in English I still could not understand what he was saying.

The night after, 6th July, I noticed there was no spirit activity. It was very quiet and on the Saturday I was pleased to say that it remained peaceful.

Spirit was telling me that their friends had been helped and taken to the world of spirit.

I travelled back to England on the Sunday. As soon as I returned home I phoned my friend Midge to see how she was and on the Monday I took her to hospital for more radium treatment on the cancer, Midge was to remain in hospital then for several weeks. She was very ill.

Towards the end of July Midge was moved to Musgrove

Hospital at Taunton. Her health was deteriorating and she was in much pain.

On the 29th July I attended a special occasion at Blue Cross Church. Bill and Julie (members of my group) had a son David, and it was his naming ceremony, this is similar to a christening, but is adapted to the spiritualist movement. Whilst there I could see many spirit friends who had come to join in with the ceremony. It was a wonderful feeling, both for the people on the earth plane and our friends in spirit.

On the 3rd August whilst taking my group, Allan was taken over in trance by a guide and the guide spoke to us all. This was the first time Allan had ever experienced it. I would just like to say that it can happen to anyone if they are prepared to work at it for genuine reasons, we managed to record what his helpers had to say and we discussed afterwards how Allan had felt throughout this talk. Allan felt the energy rising from his stomach area up to his throat, he was aware of the words he was saying but not where he was getting them from. At the beginning he felt that if he had swallowed he would have lost this link, this was spirits way of giving Allan the choice.

On the 14th August, I attended Bridgwater Spiritualist Church to give a talk and demonstration on healing, Midge came with me but this time she was in a wheelchair, she had only been allowed out of hospital for a short period of time, something that I felt moved about was Midge had explained to everyone how the healing she received had helped her; although it had not cured her, it kept her going on for so much longer. It had also given her a better understanding for when she was to pass to spirit. She knew exactly what to expect and was spiritually prepared. Her words touched everyone that day.

On the 19th August I took Midge, again, to Bridgwater Church. Unfortunately, I felt that this would be the last time that Midge would attend as she was so ill, this I was so saddened by.

August passed, without much happening although I found another Church at Bridgwater, which happened to be a Christian Spiritualist Church.

On the 6th September, I visited Glastonbury Abbey again and whilst I was sitting on the grass, meditating, I became aware that I could see the Abbots and Monks of ages past, walking through the grounds singing hymns, although I could not make out exactly what was being sung.

I attended another psychic supper at Bridgwater Church on the 8th September. Again, it left me with the same opinion; it is so difficult to work under these conditions, it amazes me that some people do attempt it.

My friend Midge, was now in St Margaret's Hospice at Taunton and I had visited her on several occasions but on each visit she was slipping further and further away.

On the 10th September 1990 I felt a significant change must be made where in place of my garage I must have a Sanctuary built; a place of peace where healing could be given, not only for myself but for others, also the teaching of various spiritual aspects conducted by people who have a gift from spirit who were prepared to pass on their knowledge in order that they may not only help themselves but help others develop too.

On Wednesday 12th September, I was attending a demon-stration at Belgrave Square by a Medium called Bill Lloyd. I received a message quite sharp and to the point, Bill told me that I was not from this area but from a Sanctuary somewhere, I was very surprised by this and it takes a lot to surprise me, I can tell you. He said I had a lot of work to do in it and needed to return home. This again was more confirmation to me.

On Friday 14th September 1990 my very dear friend, Midge, passed away to spirit. Everyone who knew her was saddened by her loss.

My group met that night and as we all sat around my table we became aware of a Nun, she had come to tell us that she had taken Midge to her resting place, it was then that I made my mind up that my Sanctuary would be dedicated to Midge, for the love she had given to others, right through to the end. I would have it opened and blessed by Dot Matthews (another person who was very close to my heart) and everyone who visits my was. Midge, when she passed, left her husband and a young son Oliver, who sadly miss her.

The following day, 15th September, I was asked to give a talk at a Psychic Fair in Wells (as you are aware, my feelings towards these are that the demonstrators do not work on the right vibrations). I attended it thinking there might be someone whom I could help, only three people came to my talk and I talked and demonstrated to them hoping that they would benefit from it, as you watch it becomes quite obvious that people only want clairvoyance but to me healing is a far greater gift.

That night I attended a talk and demonstration at Weston-super-Mare. I was immediately put off when the Medium came on to the platform, she had her dog with her and she let it sit on her lap, throughout much of the service it licked her face. It is my own feeling that if Mediums are to do their work they surely don't need their dog with them on the platform and can leave them at home if they are the ones that are demonstrating (even if they do believe it's the dog giving them the power). By all means we welcome animals into our Sanctuary and Church, especially for healing, but not if its off-putting.

Another member of my group, Doug, had been given a task by me of building a pyramid out of cardboard, he was to make it large enough for a person to sit in and after a service one Sunday night, a group of us went round to Doug and Beryl's house to look at the pyramid and we each took turns to sit in it. Midge made contact with us, through Allan and explained that she was doing fine and she would communicate with us again.

An Indian and other guides also came to speak to us through Allan whilst he sat in the pyramid.

On the Sunday morning I attended Blue Cross Church and in the afternoon Wells Spiritualist Church, I received messages at both of these, it did not surprise me as I find I usually receive a message wherever I go. On my mind, all that day, was the memory of the time that I had travelled with Midge and Dot to the church yard in Hempsted near Gloucester, where Canon Charles is buried, (he had served this Church for several years, prior to his death). Canon Charles is one of the helpers who often comes to talk to us through Dot and at times I am given him in various messages at the Churches that I attend, I always acknowledge him and thank him wherever he appears.

On Wednesday 19th September 1990, Midge was cremated. Monica Russell conducted the service at Weston-super-Mare Cremetorium and asked me to help her by saying a few words. Many of Midge's friends were there, those who knew her will never forget her. The feelings of sadness and such a great loss of a very dear friend were strong that day. Lil had seen Midge spiritually standing alongside me as I spoke about her. I would like to share these words with you:

'Death is nothing at all - I have only slipped away into the next room.
I am I, and you are you.
Whatever we were to each other, that we still are.
Call me by my old familiar name, speak to me in the easy way which you always used.
Put no difference in your tone, wear no forced air of solemnity or sorrow.
Laugh as we always laughed at the little jokes we enjoyed together.
Let my name be ever the household word that it always was, let it be spoken without effect, without the trace of a shadow on it.
Life means all that it ever meant.
It is the same as it ever was; there is unbroken continuity.
Why should I be out of mind because I am out of sight?
I am waiting for you, for an interval, somewhere very near, just around the corner.
All is well'.

Henry Scott Holland 1847-1918
Canon at St Pauls Cathedral

As September went on I looked around for a builder that could build my Sanctuary. I soon found one, Martin Perry. He was huge man with a heart full of gold.

On September 22nd my Sanctuary was started, first of all my garage had to be knocked down, and the base laid. As the days and weeks went by my Sanctuary began to take shape, it wasn't too big, it wasn't too small. I knew what I wanted in it and I knew what atmosphere I wanted to create there.

We soon got into October and I travelled to London to visit some friends. We eventually finished up at Belgrave Square to watch an evening demonstration, the lady Medium conducting the demonstration was very nicely dressed and came across very well, but to me anyone who is going to demonstrate clairvoyancy (especially somewhere like Belgrave Square), needs to be capable of linking directly to the individual they are with, and this lady to me could not. She started by opening up the message 'who can take'. I don't like this when I see a Medium working this way. I feel they could put a little more effort into it to know who they are with. How many times can we take or accept a message what is being given to somebody else? Surely this is where training and discipline comes into how any Medium works, the Medium should be fully capable of forming that link.

After six or seven messages given in this way she started giving another one and I soon realised that she was with me, but I am sorry, I will never claim a message at any demonstration or Church regardless of who the Medium is, that is just me being stubborn. It is important that they reach me direct and not leave the message wide open. How many of us could actually claim a message what we hear in a Church even though it's not for us? When this Medium realised she was with me she said to me,

'I am with you',

'I know' I said.

She asked, 'why have you not claimed it?'

so I replied, 'I will not claim messages in that way as that method is not good enough.'

The lady got quite annoyed with me because I had actually answered her back, she told me that her helpers used to work that way where they went to the individual but they don't now. So I replied I felt that she needed to discuss it with her helpers and look at what is best for the people. The lady proceeded to give a message which I could link with but I don't think she has forgiven me to this day for disagreeing with her method in front of the public that were there. To me it was obvious she was working on a materialistic link anyway, which I felt needed pointing out.

Towards the third week of October, I was travelling up to Teeside and called at Dukinfield to see my parents. I also visited Denton Church while I was there. I saw a friend of mine who I had met several months before called Kay (we would sit and talk about spiritual work whenever we could meet) and she told me that my card had dropped out of her bag four days before as if to tell her that I was on my way.

I received a small message that night whilst at Denton from a lady Medium who told me that there was a Monk with me, he was lifting his habit up to show his sandals. What I had discovered some time before was that each Monk 'Order' wear different sandals; the straps go differently on their feet or in between their toes, thus showing the Order that they came from. I unfortunately cannot recognise the variations, but I believe this information may be useful at sometime.

I travelled between Teeside and Dukinfield for nearly a month while attending a fire service course at Teeside Airport. I would visit the various Churches at weekends that I wouldn't often get the opportunity to. One Sunday, towards the end of October, I was in a small Church and I watched the chairman walk in, I was thoroughly disappointed with him. He was dressed as if he had just come out of the garden, with his polo neck sweater, scruffy trousers and no polish on his shoes. I personally think it is quite important that whoever is chairing bothers to come over dressed smartly and presentable. I am not saying they have to have new clothes – I am just saying they should come over nicely dressed, this is one of my problems as I do tend to be picky and I am particular but if you are working for spirit – come on, let us at least show willing and dress accordingly and put more effort into our appearance.

As I was making my way home in November, I called at Pocklington to see Madge. I discovered that one of her gifts was rescue work (where you help the lost souls that have remained earth-bound instead of passing to the world of spirit). Normally it would take a group of people to help such spirits but Madge did it on her own and was quite capable of doing this well. I learnt a lot from her that afternoon about rescue work and how to help the earth-bound spirits. Please recognise that only specialised people are capable of doing this work as they know the dangers involved. You must understand at this stage, that as we develop our spirit helpers develop with us.

Our spirit guides can be on different levels, they choose to be with us but also they can learn from our actions.

Despite popular belief, our spirit helpers are not capable of knowing everything, their knowledge varies from guide to guide just like ours does from person to person, except our guides work within a team; if they do not know an answer to our question or cannot give us as much protection as we need, they will find a helper who can. Which is why I feel it necessary to say that only skilled people in the field of rescue can do this safely, as they have the required guides and helpers giving them the knowledge and protection they need when helping earth-bound spirits.

On the Saturday night, after church in Denton, I called for a drink in a local pub with Kay, whilst sat there I became aware that spirit was telling me something about the carpet in the pub, it turned out to be that this carpet was the type of carpet I needed for my Sanctuary; many colours, bright and hard wearing. I remembered this.

I eventually got back home on the 5th November. I had been away for nearly a month and my Sanctuary was starting to take shape. The walls were beginning to go up slowly, the window frames in, the base was obviously down and you could see that a lot of thought was being put into it by Martin, I felt very honoured that at long last my Sanctuary was beginning to take shape.

CHAPTER NINE

DEDICATION

A week later I travelled to Luton to meet a friend of mine, Billy Elton. Billy is a well known Medium in the Bedford area; he is about 80, looks 60 and my word, he was good at his work!

Billy had sat in a circle for ten years without getting anything at all, eventually his dedication paid off when one day he attended a Church where the Medium did not bother to turn up, so Billy was told that he must take the service by members of the Church. From that day everything has fitted into place and he's never looked back since. He works on a very fast vibration, which means he reaches many people in a short period of time, he's been in the movement for 45 years and is still as cheeky as the day he started, even though he is a Minister of the S.N.U!

I also got the opportunity of visiting Churches whilst I was there and he took me to his own Spiritualist Church at Aylesbury where he chaired and I can honestly say that I have never seen anybody chair as well as he did. He was brilliant. He put everything into it, love, skill, everything.

Early in December I travelled up to Watford to visit my friend Marie, as it was her grandson's barmitzvah, and whilst driving there I became aware of Midge with me in the car, so strong and she was tickling my face to tell me that she was there. I felt really pleased that she had made contact with me again. So I told her to sit down in her seat and enjoy the ride, not float around my head!

On the Friday night I gave healing to a lady called Dee, who happened to be a good friend of Marie's. Everything was getting prepared for the barmitzvah and on the Saturday we all travelled to a Synagogue to watch their ceremony. It was very interesting to see a Jewish barmitzvah and we returned back afterwards to Marie's hotel. I suddenly started feeling ill. I was being drained physically and mentally quite rapidly and no matter how much I asked for protection it was not strong enough to stop whatever was doing it to me. At first I thought it was somebody there. I had to leave the hotel and sit down. It took me several hours to recover but there was nobody there, who had done it to me, that I could see.

That night I picked up that it was a man that had done this to me and the man was not there at all. He was somewhere else but I did not know where, and I knew that he had to be very strong to be able to do it to me with the protection that I would normally have.

I gave out a few of my cards whilst I was at Watford to just a couple of people who needed help and healing (Dee being one of them).

On the Monday I travelled back to Dukinfield to visit my parents and of course, I got the opportunity to visit the different Churches there. I met my friend Kay again, and we had a good talk, she told me about a friend of hers that needed help as she was having problems with a spirit form in her home. This spirit was upsetting her young child and the child was frightened of going to bed in a certain room. This spirit was quite strong and capable of lifting the covers off the bed, moving the furniture and making noises. They were all very aware that it was in the house, so I made arrangements to go and see this young girl the following day.

That night I wrote some Christmas cards and when I wrote Dee's I put in another healing card for some reason, which is very unusual because normally I don't give anyone two, but for some reason I had to put another one in with her Christmas card.

The following day I got the opportunity to go and visit this young girl who lived in a small terraced house in Denton, and when I went in and talked to her she explained how this spirit had been troubling them for some time. For some reason I could hear a baby crying, but it must have been a spirit baby because there was no baby in the house at the time, just the woman. I explained to her that I would go upstairs to this one particular room to see if I could sense anything or pick anything up. I went into the small back bedroom where the baby would normally sleep, it was a beautifully coloured bedroom. All the toys were hanging from the ceiling and a cot was in the corner. Although the room still had a very cold feeling about it she told me that whatever heat they put in there they could not warm it up. I sat on a chair and waited for a few minutes and very soon became aware of a spirit forming. This spirit turned out to be a man and I communicated with him and asked him why he was being like he was, he explained to me that the house had been his home and he was a bit mischievious. He needed help to get to the spirit world and it had been him, that had drained me on the Saturday. He had done this to find out what I was aware of and if I was capable of helping him. I was lost for words when he told me this, so I said a prayer for him and told him that I would help him. I asked my helpers to come along and help him into the world of spirit. He was very grateful and I shook hands with him in friendship even though he was a spirit form, and then we both left.

That night I discovered that Dee had been to hospital during the day and they had found a lump in her chest which they thought was cancer and she would have to have it removed at some later date.

I managed to do another talk and demonstration at Hyde Church that week. About fifteen to twenty people attended but again I got a nice feeling. The girl that runs it, Maria, put so much into it. She is such a good worker for spirit and I do wish more people would recognise it, but they are unaware of her gifts and do not understand.

On the 17th December I had a very unusual phone call, it was to tell me that Dee had gone into hospital that day to have her lump removed and she was holding my healing card against her chest as she was going down to the theatre. The print had come out of the card on to her chest so when they came to operate the lump had gone completely, and so had the design on the card (this was the reason I had sent her the second card). She now always carries both cards with here, the one where the ink had run and the new one.

On the 18th December I had my carpet fitted in the Sanctuary and I gave my good friends and neighbours, Den and Mary Sweet, healing. They were the first ones I had given healing to in my Sancturary, it was so lovely to be able to repay my good friends back for all the help they had given me.

On the 19th December I went to visit Martin (the builder) and his wife Mo, to give them a Christmas card and just before I went I asked spirit which one I should give them. I had bought some

Den and Mary receiving healing in my Sanctuary

Sanctuary

from the hospice where Midge had been that were special. They were of a design with a star on. Whilst I was talking to Mo she told me a story of how she was attending to her father-in-law who was dying, this continued for a while. When he eventually passed and she left the hospital, in the sky was this great big star. She told me that this star will always remind her of her father-in-law as it was shining so bright. I told her to open the Christmas card and have a look. This she did and she has still not got over it to this day, as the card bears the star which is the link she has with her father-in-law.

My Sanctuary was finished a week before Christmas and I felt so pleased; it had exposed beams in the ceiling, I had bought a stereo so that I could always have music in there, I had various lights all around the ceiling (which were operated by dimmer switches), these reflected against the blue of the walls and the white ceiling. It was only 23 feet long and 12 feet wide but I felt that there was so much work to be done in there, after all size is not important.

I travelled up to Dukinfield on Christmas Eve and attended the midnight mass at an ordinary Church. I realised that I could see spirit forms of all the clergy who had obviously served there throughout the years that the Church had been going. They were all stood at the side of the Church waiting patiently as the service took place. I wondered how the others would react if they could see them, and it made me appreciate my gift that little bit more.

When I got home I had a look then at my own development and in such a short period of time I had become aware of spirits so much from sensing that I could now 'see' as well. I get my signal quite clearly and my healing capabilities are building up as each day goes along. I don't always see and I quite often pick various things up with different people to give them a small message. I thank spirit every day for using me and teaching me and ask them to continue to do so.

I had a message whilst in Bridgwater Church from Monica Russell (who was the President at that time). Part of the message was a small warning to watch my step and be careful. I never thought any more about it.

On the 29th December I was preparing to have my Sanctuary opened and dedicated (I had asked Dot Matthews to come down from Gloucester to do it for me). I had a ladder against my house to get some furniture out of the bedroom window (as they would not fit down the stairs) to put in the Sanctuary. The ladder slipped and I fell, but as luck would have it I did not hurt myself even though I had to change my 'clothes', and then I remembered the message I had received the week before. 'Watch my step and be careful'.

Eighteen people attended the opening of my Sanctuary. All very good friends I had met as I went on my travels. Dot Matthews was absolutely brilliant. I found it was so difficult to talk especially about my friend Midge as tears were streaming down my face because I wanted all these people to know about her (like I want everyone that comes to my Sanctuary to know about her). The service took about an hour and a half and it created a lovely warm feeling and everybody was overjoyed and very emotional. My son, Steven, had prepared us some food and afterwards we continued in to the house where we still talked about the service.

When everyone had gone home that night, we held our first circle within the Sancturary. Dot Matthews, Hillary, Allan and Kay who were all very close friends. We all sat around the large oblong table (which I have in my Sanctuary) and we started off with a prayer, Dot talked to us for a while before going into trance and then some of her spirit helpers talked through her, and gave each one of us various messages and information. If only more people could work the way Dot does, with her helpers, so many people could be helped and given proof of survival after death.

NOTES AND FEELINGS

CHAPTER TEN

DOLPHINS

At the start of the New Year (1991), I sat in my Sanctuary for a short while just to remember what had gone on the year previously. I was now up to 125 tapes of various messages which I had been given from all kinds of Mediums, they give me quite a lot of knowledge which is what I wanted, and I was looking forward to 1991 to see what form of spiritual experiences I would have this year and how I would react as a human being when they happened to me.

There is no such thing as time in the spirit world, it is only us on the earth plane that recognise time as '24 hours in the day'. Quite often when people pass into the world of spirit they do not communicate with us for many of 'our' years, often they do not realise how our time has passed as they too are learning to communicate between both worlds.

So, please, do not feel disheartened if you don't receive a message from your loved ones for a long time after they have passed over.

One of the last messages I had received from a Medium told me that someone was coming to visit me. This someone would travel from London to see my Sanctuary. At this time I did not have a clue who it was but within a week they appeared, it was a lady from the London area, Stevie, she had travelled up to see me to talk about healing and spiritual work as she had done a lot of work with aromatherapy; healing and counselling.

I know you might find it hard to believe, but between all these journeys and trips I was still continuing to work as a fireman at the airport, and sometimes when I had a few hours to myself I would play the tapes and write them out into various books for some reason. Who knows, maybe someone would want to read them one day.

January had almost past and I still visited many places. I was beginning to get feedback from people who had been using my card and asking for help, that they were receiving it and feeling better. I found that I had the capability of talking to people about healing, how it worked and how it happened. It gave them so much more than understanding. I also find that often people come my way who are good Healers, although they do not know it, and they just need that knowledge and help to put them on the right pathway which is what we should all be doing. We should be helping others to develop that gift and not holding them back, so many times I've seen it where somebody had a particular gift, either Healing or Mediumship, and they are not allowed to develop because someone holds them back.

So many times on your pathway you will meet egotistical people that will hold you back, as they see what gift you have and don't let you develop it in case you are better than them. It is my intention to take people up to a stage within their development and then pass them on to someone who would be able to further their knowledge better than myself. It doesn't bother me that this person may be a far greater Healer or Medium than myself.

It was the end of January before I got the opportunity for my group to meet. There was only six of us that night when we met in the Sancturary, we talked about the protection we all needed, we had a small meditation and gave each other healing, again recognising that we too can receive healing as well as give.

I was sat in my cottage one night, just resting when my cats and I heard a spirit walk down the stairs, so I welcomed it and thanked it for visiting me although I could not see it. I was not frightened at all, it was a pleasant experience and I acknowledged it.

Towards the end of February Dot Matthews came to my Sanctuary to give a demonstration on clairvoyance. I invited a few of the people I had met within the last few weeks so they could come and watch her. They were more than pleased with what they heard and I had feedback from that evening coming for several weeks afterwards.

I had given one of my healing cards to a work colleague's wife and she had taken it with her to an old lady she knew who suffered terribly with her hands from arthritis and the lady was not able to hold anything with both hands let alone one. They told me that they gave that lady the card and held her hands together with it between them. The lady could feel the warmth and the heat coming out of the card and afterwards she was quite capable of picking a teapot up with one hand and using it. They were all pleased and did not know what to make of it at all. Again, I thanked my spirit helpers for helping that lady and asked them to continue helping her.

It's not often we get feedback on how people are helped, they just expect us 'to know' automatically. You should never feel dispondant when you do not get any feedback from people you have been helping.

In March I discovered a Spiritualist Church that I had not been to before. It was in a Quakers Meeting Hall in Taunton. The welcome you received when you went in there was overwhelming. The people were all nice and friendly and the Medium on that night was a chap called the Reverend Fred Rendle. He is the only Medium I have ever seen in a dog-collar!

It is amazing when I see the different Spiritualist Churches (and I always look at how many attend). It is one of the first things I do when I sit down – just count how many people there are there. Sometimes there may only be ten and other times as many as sixty or seventy. The age limit does seem to change in different areas of the country I am in, I have noticed that in the

North a lot more younger people seem to attend then anywhere else I have been. In other areas it is all women with very few men.

I feel we should be urgently looking at the young people of today and giving them a better understanding of our movement, we should never underestimate the youngsters of today, as they are our workers for tomorrow.

Around this time I contacted the Arthur Finlay College at Stanstead. I had heard so much about it on my travels that this was 'the place to go', and the place to learn. I applied for one of the programmes and it came in the post (there was so many fantastic courses that you could attend to learn that you were really spoilt for choice). The teacher's names I was not drawn to, just because they are well known, doesn't mean they are any good. As there was so many different courses I asked spirit to help me. I asked them to show me the course I needed to go on. As I went through the booklet I was really drawn to the German week which was taking part in early April. My mind was made up and I applied for the course, really looking forward to it. Even then the Receptionist at Stanstead tried to change my mind, by commenting on the nationality of people attending, which made me all the more determined to go.

Towards the end of March I managed to have another demonstration in my Sanctuary. This time it was taken by Sally Smith. She talked and demonstrated healing using colours and instead of touch healing she just used the energy around your body to heal. It gave the people who attended something to think about.

The day afterwards, Pat (a friend of mine), brought her sister-in-law for healing to my Sanctuary, Marjorie, who was almost totally deaf which caused me to discover that day, how difficult it was to communicate with someone who could not really hear you, it taught me so much about communication it was incredible. When I think about it, I have never seen anybody cater for deaf people at the Churches I have attended or demonstrations. There is never anybody doing sign language

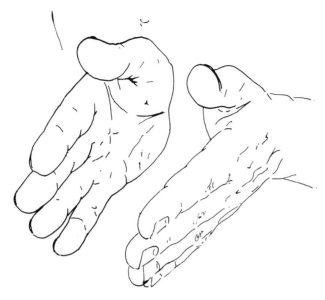

We can feel our own energies by bringing our hands slowly together, or by bringing our hands together around someone's head we can feel their energies.

and in truth you don't usually find that the people who are hard of hearing sit at the front in any case, I think this area should be looked at in more detail, in order to reach them.

On the 30th March I made my way to Stanstead. I called at a few places in Watford and Windsor on the way to see a few friends. I found there was one thing I really like as I go on my journeys to various Churches and demonstrations, I make so many nice friends, who are genuine.

I didn't know what the week would bring at Stanstead, and I had gone there to learn and was really looking forward to it. When I arrived I discovered that I was the only Englishman on the course. Although there were two English girls, Lynne and Jane (who were sisters), all the rest of the people were German, Dutch and Swiss. Somehow, Lynne, Jane and me ended up together on a table with two others, Maria and Gabriel from Munich. We all got on really well even though there was a lot to learn.

We would start off each morning with a meditation and then the tutors would set us lessons (for about an hour and a half). On the first day they gave us a meditation which involved going on a walk, this took a short period of time through various areas of the countryside until eventually we finished up on top of a mountain, where we sat for a few minutes, when an animal would appear out of the trees, you would have a good look at this animal, to see what his habits were (in all kinds of ways), and to see what people thought of this particular animal. Then you returned back (in the meditation) and came back to where you had started. The object of this meditation was the animal you described was actually yourself. It turned out to be very interesting and enjoyable. Everyone found that the animal they saw was a reflection of their own self, this was taken by a girl called Gerry who was one of the tutors, I felt she worked very well.

There were various talks and demonstrations that went on until late at night which were all worthwhile.

From day one we also worked in small groups of five (with the idea being that by the end of the week we would be working on a one to one basis). The first day all five of the group sat around in a small circle together, and had to tune in to one of the individuals present without telling them, we would then ask to go and have a look at their home, for certain things within it and then we would have a look at the individual to see what made them 'tick'. It was a very successful exercise. I tuned into a young girl from Germany and picked up her home and the position of the stairs, basically all that was in her house and how the house overlooked many others, I discovered that she had a lot of love within and people did not really understand her, I also picked up she was a young mother and various other points. What I found interesting was that three of the group had tuned into me; they had picked up my cottage, my two cats, they picked up the pictures which I had got on my walls (and other things as well), I found this really impressive.

We watched a man called Leonard demonstrate that night as he was one of the other tutors at Stanstead. He came over quite well, and a few of us picked up on his attitude towards various subjects.

As the week progressed yet another exercise came our way. This time we would sit in front of one another and have a look at a ball of wool that we visualised on each other's lap. We would then have a look at the thickness of this wool, the texture, colour and just what this wool was doing. Again, this wool would tell us about the individual, and we were able to tell just how their life was going at that present time (Another interesting and worthwhile exercise).

Gaye (who was running the course) gave us a demonstration involving sand reading, where sand is prepared in a tray then an individual places their hand on the sand, leaving an impression, the Medium then proceeds to give a reading from this. I had never seen that before and again it was very worthwhile and she made a good job of it.

When the Thursday arrived it was my turn to pair off with a young blonde girl, Bridget, in our class with the idea that one had a problem and the other needed help to solve it for them. This young girl told me how she constantly dreams of dolphins

Corner Cottage

113

and I realised, whilst we were talking, that she had to go to her dolphins and find them. I asked her that when she did to send me a card to say she had got there and everything was OK.

I also picked up a young man in the spirit world that used to go to school with her who had passed at a very early age and she was overwhelmed with this message. Tears of joy streamed down her face and she gave me a big hug to say thank you.

During the time I was at Stanstead, I met a few more people who needed absent healing, Jane, one girl in particular, was in the early stage of pregnancy and her baby was not lying right, before the end of the week the baby had moved to its correct position in the womb.

Just as the week was finishing one of the German men came to me and showed me something we could do with our hands. If you put your left hand on top of your right with it touching, over the area where someone is bleeding (without touching it), it will stop the bleeding and if you know that there is infection or dirt in the wound and you need to make it bleed to cleanse it, you reverse your hands so that the left hand is underneath (again, without touching). I thought this was absolutely marvellous. If you look at the way we are in this life with Aids and Hepatitis A and B, so many other diseases we can catch from the blood source by just simply touching. This technique sounded incredible and I could not wait to try it out. The man said that even the children in Germany use this method when they cut themselves, it disappoints me to think that people here in Britain are so far behind.

It was a very sad day when the course eventually broke up at the end of the week. I had made so many friends and had discovered that all the people there that week left us standing as they were so spiritual and genuine, almost unspoilt, I hoped that I would meet some of them again (I do not know where or when but I look forward to it). The friendships I had built up that week I hoped would last forever. I knew that Maria (one particular girl from Munich), would become a very good Healer. The two English girls would each go their own way but they both had their own gifts they could use which would be important not only for them but also for others that they would help.

The tutors went on their own way and I hope that they also learnt something from that week as it was quite obvious to everyone they did not get on well with each other, and to me they underestimated that their students would pick it up. You should never underestimate a student.

I had a few messages that week and one of them was from a chap called Phillip who worked as a Medium in Belgrave Square and at Stanstead but he put so much love into the way he worked, everyone noticed it. Part of the message was that I would be travelling to Scotland and all the Germans cottoned on to this one and kept asking me all week when was I going, but I did not know.

I went back to work on the Monday which was difficult; I must admit. I had been given now for over two years that I would be retiring as a fireman to devote my life as a Healer and Teacher but to me there was no signs of this. They were beginning to introduce more stringent requirements in the airport fire service and as I wore glasses I could see this would create a problem.

At work as a fireman, I would often talk to people about healing and give healing to other fireman whilst at work if time allowed.

I feel it's important to mention that whilst being a fireman, I was also the airport's convener (a high position in the Union), representing all the manual workers. As I spiritually progressed, I knew more and more that I would have to give all this up, as it was beginning to conflict with my views.

I think I have mentioned there are Healers and Feelers. Unfortunately, I was told of a case where there had been some discrepencies whilst healing was being given and apparently it had been going on for some time with this particular couple. It's a shame as it gives everyone a bad name. So please remember if you do not get the right feelings off anybody when you go for healing, stop them and leave. Don't carry on and make sure you tell someone, it is important that you report anyone who is not genuine. There is no time for them in this movement, as they don't do anyone any good.

CHAPTER ELEVEN

IGNORANCE IS BLISS

I got the opportunity again in April, of working with Dot on the platform in Stroud, she was doing a demonstration of clairvoyance and I was allowed to give a ten minute talk on healing before she began, it went down well and I was invited back to give a demonstration on healing. I thanked Dot for allowing me to assist her, there are few Mediums who will allow you to share a platform nowadays, especially when you are learning. But what a better way to learn than with a skilled and qualified Medium who has their own gifts.

Here again, ego rears it's ugly head, as Mediums do not like sharing a platform, just in case you give a message better than their own and the audience appreciates you more than that Medium, especially when you are only training or learning. This shouldn't be so, after all we're supposed to be working together for the benefit of mankind, not against one another.

I ran my first day course involving a healing talk and demonstration which lasted all day in my Sanctuary. I covered many areas of healing and the problems we may encounter as Healers. Twelve people came and it was all very hectic, I did feel that it took it out of me but it went down really well. I learnt a lot and I hope that the people who attended learnt also. I gave healing and everybody had a go themselves.

Dot Matthews was down that night to do a demonstration on clairvoyance. She had given me some daffodils for my Sanctuary (in memory of her husband Alf) and as the day went on the daffodils changed shape so when night came everyone passed comment on the yellow roses that were in the vase. The yellow daffodils had changed shape completely into roses, the only difference being that there were no thorns on the stems. I knew that this was the work of Spirit and I was pleased that I had the opportunity of actually seeing and understanding what had gone on, although this didn't stop me from being amazed, even the others couldn't believe it!

At the end of April I was drawn to write to the Psychic Newspaper expressing concern about the image that was being created within our Spiritualist Churches. It is so important to be made welcome when you come into one. It may be your first time and you may not be sure where you can sit, someone should welcome you and greet you. Then as the service takes its natural course the chairperson (when they are on the platform with the Medium) needs to come across in a firm but nice way explaining how to receive a message. They need to be dressed respectably, and come across clearly to ensure that everyone within the Church understands them. They need to greet anyone who is there for the first time, not only the regulars. They need to ensure that they have got complete control over everything that goes on within the service, and to be able to cope with anything that may crop up out of the blue but unfortunately they don't. So I wrote to Psychic News expressing my views and I got some nice replies in the paper to it agreeing that I was right. I do think we need to introduce more of a professional standard within our Churches and demonstrations to ensure that we come across in a clear, precise way.

A lady came to my Sanctuary asking if she could have healing for her ulcerated legs. She had this problem for sixteen to twenty years and there was nothing anyone could do for her. I decided to use my hands (in the same way that I would use them to stop bleeding). Later she returned for healing and told me that her

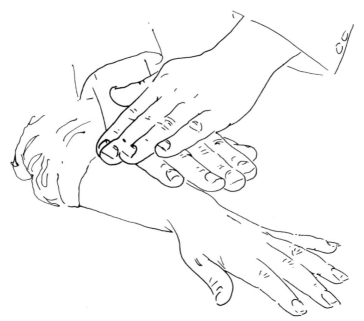

TO STOP BLEEDING, left hand over right

TO CLEANSE THE CUT, right hand over left

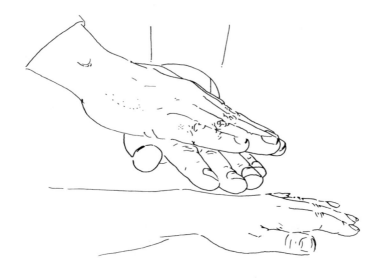

legs were doing really well. They were beginning to heal from the inside not the outside which is what was required. She had shown her doctor and the nurses, they all could not believe that after all that time they had now started to heal. I never heard from this lady again so I don't know how she got on. This often happens; you help someone and after a course of time they stop coming and you don't know if it is because they got better or they have lost interest. It may be sometime later, years even, when you bump into them and they say,

'oh yes, I have never had any trouble since you gave me the healing',

or, 'I thought you knew'.

But of course, we don't know. We can never say to anyone, 'yes, we can heal you'.

We can only help and we are just used as an instrument.

I discovered that my healing itself was developing in a productive way. Patience again being the hardest lesson I had to learn. People would come for healing and I would never ask them what their problem was as I needed my Helpers to teach me their problem. Many times I was successful in picking up what was wrong with them (although sometimes I did not get anything at all). I would feel their pain or sensation that they were experiencing at times, and, as my development progressed at certain times I would see their body as a skeleton and the area within their body where the problem lay highlighted within. There were times when I would just be given a condition like cancer or kidney problems – the words would be given to me (I did not hear those being said but I sensed them). I would always make sure my patients beforehand understood fully what was going to take place and that there would never be any guarantee that they could be healed but they would be helped. Yes, the age of the miracle is still around but normally it would take a course of healing to help them.

Some people would feel heat out of my hands. One hand may be hot and one hand may be cold. Depending on what was needed in that area of the body was what the individual would receive. I would never charge for any of these services, but I do leave a bowl for donations. If you try this simple exercise: sit down on a nice chair, get comfortable and place your right hand above your left knee. Don't touch it. Keep it about an inch away and hold it there for about two to three minutes. Now put your left hand where your right hand was and move your right hand away completely. Again, keep your left hand there for about two to three minutes. What you are looking for is a different form of sensation within your hands or within your knee. It may be hot or cold, it may feel like pins and needles or static electricity. You may not feel anything at all but don't worry. I am trying to show you the difference in your hands; One hand 'gives' and one hand 'takes' when giving healing. You would normally find that the hand which gives is the hand that you write with, but it does not always work that way so do not worry. Just see if you can feel something as you try this simple exercise. Again, this was something I had learnt at Stanstead.

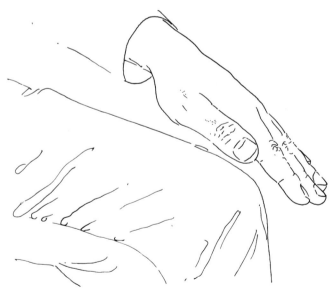

Hold your right hand over your knee for a few minutes then change hands using the same knee, note the difference in energies.

I had some friends turn up from Bristol for healing. The first time I ever gave them healing, Bernard actually lifted his arm up and put it behind his neck, he told me that for two years he had not been able to lift that arm more than six or seven inches from his body and after the first time of healing he actually put it behind his neck which he thought was amazing. Again, I thanked my Helpers and told him to carry on coming as he still had a few more problems which he needed help with.

In June I got the opportunity of travelling with the Bristol and Somerset Healers Association to the Harry Edwards Sanctuary at Sheer and what a magnificent home! The two people that run it, Ray and Joan Branch, met the group when we arrived and showed us around. I felt pleased that I had made this journey and to see where the great man had worked for many years and I knew of what work he had done there and how many people he had helped, I also knew that he was still working with so many people from the world of spirit.

My friend Lorraine Davies had moved to Bristol now, she was working as a graphologist within the area and we started communicating again it was really good to speak to an old friend. I continued having demonstrations of clairvoyance whenever I could, within my Sancturary. Dot Matthews would usually do one for me if I asked. Also, towards the end of June, Lorraine Davies did me a workshop on graphology and mediumship, which went down very well. Again, it is something else to look at and something else to learn from, you need to go along with what you feel happy with – that is what is important.

I also got the opportunity of going to see Matthew Manning at Bristol Cancer Help Centre. Matthew has got his own Sanctuary and has travelled all over the world. He is quite famous. I watched him that night whilst he did his talk and demonstration, but to be honest, I expected more, because I had thought I would learn more from a man with such a gift as he had. I met a friend there who I had not seen for such a long time and she told me that she had cancer so she started coming to my Sanctuary for a few weeks. I had never met such a person with so much willpower to live and survive as she did, she had many operations and travelled around the country to different hospitals to see how they could help her. The healing helped her in a way to carry on fighting but it did not remove the cancer as you may expect, although it gave her the courage and strength to carry on.

People would come to my Sanctuary to talk about healing, clairvoyance and spiritual work and I find that no matter how long you spend with them you can never cover enough. The same with my group and the demonstrations you could talk until the early hours of the morning but what we all must realise is that we do need time to ourselves. I find that every single day when I am not working I would be spending time with Spirit, helping people because I love doing it. I get the satisfaction when someone says 'thank you, I appreciate what you have done for me'. That means so much. If someone was to give me a thousand pounds it would not mean the same as someone simply saying thank you.

I had another interesting experience where I met a friend of mine, Mo, she explained to me that all her life she had had problems with her hands where the heat would build up and be really uncomfortable. I told her that when this happened, to send out the heat as I believed it was healing building up within, she should pass it on to people who needed help. We actually met at a street fair in Wedmore when we began talking about this. All of a sudden her hands started getting hot and within a few minutes she had the opportunity of passing that healing on as we were joined by some other friends, one of them had been in a road traffic accident I told her before to put her hand on this woman's shoulders and watch, sure enough the heat went down as the energy was removed from Mo to the other person who needed the help. At one time Mo had even considered an operation to remove the glands in her hands but luckily the surgeon had refused to do this and now whenever Mo gets the sensation coming on she sends out that healing and her hands cool down. I had never heard of anything like this before.

In July I travelled to Blackpool for a week with the Transport and General Workers Union for a conference and each evening I got the opportunity of visiting a different Church within that area to see what I thought. On the Sunday I went to Blackpool Church and was very disappointed whilst receiving a message that the chairperson interrupted the Medium to tell him it was the last message. This, of course, put him off track and my message stopped short. This should never have happened, a chairperson should have the respect to wait until a Medium has finished giving a message, to speak, even whether it's about time, after all, it's a simple courtesy.

I went to Cleevely Spiritualist Church on the Monday (a house that had been converted into a Church). I felt a very nice feeling and the people were also friendly. More than twenty people attended the service that night and I thought it went very well.

On the Tuesday I visited Fleetwood Church. The lady Medium there 'gave off' and there was also an open circle afterwards, which, to my shock over one hundred and twenty people attended. I had never seen that many in an open circle. I felt there was far too many for that, but the Medium did well, giving several messages, it is good though, to see so much interest.

On the Wednesday night, I visited St Annes Church (this was a Pensioner's Hall). There was a lady called Billy Hallowell giving a service on 'flower sensitive'. (I met her and her friend Carol that night). But all I had brought for the service as regards a flower, was a weed which had been growing outside the Church (because I had not realised it was a flower service). Billy gave a message from the platform and said that whoever's flower she held, their healing was going all over the world. I thought it was good to get some form of confirmation.

The following Friday night, I did a talk and demonstration on healing at Dukinfield Church (the Church where I had been to as a small boy with my father). About twenty-five people attended and I had a very good response from them. I got over a hundred names for my healing book. When the demonstration finished I realised that one young woman had a problem which she had not talked about and so I asked her what it was. She told me that she had a boy and a girl aged 12 and 14 who both suffered from allopecia and they were losing their hair, this was quite seriously affecting all of them. On the Saturday morning I went around to their house and gave all three of them healing.

The Sunday I received a telephone call whilst at my parents and I was asked if I would do the service that night at Dukinfield Church. Words cannot really express my feelings that day as it was a dream I had always had; being able to serve that Church, as it had served me many years before. I went and did my first healing service in the Church. This was the 14th July 1991. I hoped that night I reached many people. I know I definitely gave them something to think about with my talk on philosophy. Instead of giving Mediumship I gave healing and told the audience what I was picking up with them. I was invited back so it must have been a success.

I was still communicating with some of the friends I had met at Stanstead. Jane now lived in Germany as her husband was in the Forces there, and Maria still lived in Munich. They were all doing well although Jane had had a few problems with her baby so she had asked me to continue sending her healing which I did, and the problems were soon put right.

Two people came for healing at the end of July, Gwen and Cora. Gwen had a tumour on the brain. I gave her healing and she said that the pressure she felt had eased and she was not in so much pain. They came for just a few days and during that time we talked about healing, death and the spirit world as I felt it was necessary. I thought they needed to understand, after healing she was not in as much pain, but her problem was still there.

My group was progressing very well. The Guides were now talking through Hillary and Allan on quite a regular basis by giving us information and allowing me to talk to them.

On Saturday 3rd August I received a card from Hawaii. It was from Bridget (the young German girl from Stanstead) she told me that she had made her way and she was now with the dolphins. She lived on Hawaii so she could be with them all the time. She thanked me for everything I had done and said how happy she was. I would never have dreamed that day at Stanstead when I gave her the message how important it was for her, and how she would travel from her home in Germany to live in Hawaii. So friends, always be aware of what you give to anyone in a message as we don't know the true extent of it, or where it would lead them.

On the 7th August Gwen passed away peacefully in her sleep. Cora asked me if I would conduct the service at the Crematorium in Bath for Gwen. I told her that I had no qualifications to do such a thing but she insisted and so I went there. I played the tranquility music that I used for healing and just talked a little bit about Gwen. The service went very well. Gwen's friends were there to say their final farewell and appreciated the talk. Cora thanked me which means everything.

A lesson we have to learn sometimes as Healers is that many people will come to us just before they pass and our job is not only to help them in their physical sense but in their spiritual sense, we need to help them understand more and prepare them for passing, to remove those worries that everyone has about dying. I often find that you get so close to an individual when you are giving them healing, as they become your friend, so when they pass it is almost like part of you goes with them. It is a very hard lesson we have to learn as we go along our pathway but it is a must, that we learn and understand it, as many times as it will come our way.

I heard of a man called Daskalos from some friends of mine in Bridgwater Church. He lives in Cyprus and I made my mind up that I was going to Cyprus to find him, as this man was so spiritual and gifted I thought I have got to find him to see what he could do, and to see if he could teach me something.

On the 13th August I received a postcard from Angelsey. It was from the woman and children to whom I had given healing a few weeks before. She told me that her girl's hair now had fully grown back to normal, and she thanked me as it had helped all of them considerably.

Jim, my ex-father-in-law, passed away in August and I attended his funeral in Dukinfield. I asked Beryl if I could say a few words at his service. It was funny, but all these years I had known him I had only come to realise what he was really like during the last twelve months. He had attended my Sanctuary and he always carried my card with him for help and healing after Gladys (his wife) had passed away. Nobody ever really understood him, I think. The vicar who was taking the service refused to stop in the Crem whilst I said a few words about him. I felt disgusted and disappointed, this is a member of the clergy who does not know everything and we were polite enough to sit and listen to what he had to say, but he was not prepared to listen to what I had to say. I feel different religions could learn a lot from ours if they actually sat and listened, but instead this vicar chose to be ignorant.

A story I can relate to you which I have heard on my journeys was of an evening demonstration one night in the Midlands. The Medium gave a man a short message. All it consisted of was an address, and when the service had finished the man went to the Medium and thanked him. He explained that he was a priest and had travelled from Italy to attend the meeting that night. As he and other fellow priests sat in a circle in their own country, a young girl would visit their circle and help them and he was told to come to England for that demonstration to get the address of where the young girl used to live which is what he had received that night. It just goes to show how and what goes on in other religions, that will often condemn our work. I hope this gives you something to think about.

Notes and Feelings

CHAPTER TWELVE

LABOUR PAINS

Another story I would like to relate to you is of a story of a man who lived on the island of Jersey. He looked out from his village one day with some others, and they allegedly could see two space ships, the UFO's flew over them and one was obviously in trouble so they landed on the hillside away from the village. Plenty of people travelled up the hillside to see what they could find. There were no signs of the space ship but when they arrived there were two large round burn marks in the gorse where something had obviously landed. Something or someone had set fire to all the gorse, to remove any signs of the burn marks. One day I bumped into Lorraine and she said to me 'Bill, all I'm getting with you is Jersey, and you will understand what I mean'. I will always think of Jersey now, with these UFO's, and look at it whenever it comes up.

In December I gave a talk and demonstration on healing at a Sanctuary in Brislington, Bristol. This Sanctuary is run by three girls: Diane, Jean and Marion, who have dedicated their lives to helping people. They were Mediums and Healers and had to have something going on within their Sanctuary every week, if it wasn't healing it was a group or discussion or a demonstration, with these three you usually find Billy Thomas (who's a well known Medium in the South West of England). All four work together and they all put so much love into everything they do, when the demonstration had finished for the night, I was invited to do a service in Frenchay for the coming year as they said it needs to be booked up that early to try to get people they can rely on. This gave me something else to look forward to even though it was a year away.

I travelled to Cyprus on the 18th September. The first three or four days I spent constantly trying to find someone who had heard of Daskalos or knew where he was. I knew he lived in Nicosia. I needed to try and get there from where I was staying but no luck and no response at all. I gave healing to some friends I met there, David and Hazel, Christina and Nick, Hazel was yet another friendship that I felt that would remain forever. She was Liverpudlian, but she worked on the island of Cyprus and I found out that whenever I was with her, I could pick up so much for her that it was incredible. I find this at times, that I come across an individual and it's so easy to be able to give them a message and you just can keep going on forever. Now wouldn't it be nice if we could pick up for everyone that we come in contact with. By contact I mean at a demonstration, private reading or at a service. I feel that when we look at it, you watch the Mediums demonstrate and if they've got an hours demonstration they may reach eight people. I've watched some Mediums give thirty people a message in an hour and a half. My aim is to be able to reach everyone immaterial of what level they are on or how they are thinking at the time. With this in mind, I intend to work on it. Whilst I was in Cyprus I also met a doctor who had his own clinic, he was also an acupuncturist. All the ladies that go to him are pregnant, if they wish, he gives them acupuncture so they don't feel any pain during labour at all, he'd been doing this for over two years and the only thing I didn't like about it was apparently all the babies that had been born following acupuncture were hyperactive. I think this is some-thing to think about ladies, should you have a painless birth and know about it every day from that day onwards? It's something that could be looked at a lot harder. He was studying every case and kept his records up-to-date as the children aged. Even though the children were hyperactive the mothers still returned for their next birth.

As I look at pregnancy, I feel it is important from the day of conception that both parents show love to their baby whilst it is in the womb (as well as when it grows up), by talking to it and stroking the woman's tummy with love and affection continually expressing their feelings for the child. The mother should find herself some peaceful music to which she can lie down to and sleep with, so she can give her feelings to the baby, telling it what she's doing and what the music is for ie: going to sleep. She needs to do this for the full term of the pregnancy then, not only will the baby react to the music and relax but she will as well. This music can then be used whilst the mother is in labour, then, as the baby grows and it needs sleep the parents can play the music to the baby, as it has learnt to associate sleep with the music. The baby should begin to relax.

The results of all these; love accompanied with music, I feel will produce a happy and contented baby.

While I was in Cyprus I met up with a Dutch couple (the woman looked just like Doris Day). We went in a landrover on safari together and I soon realised there was something special about them. Throughout the day we talked about healing and other spiritual subjects, we arranged to meet the day after, when she said she'd had a dream about me, where she'd been married to me in a previous life and we'd lived on the island of Cyprus. I had my confirmation of this whilst we were talking, and I also knew that she'd been given a lot more within that dream that she didn't say, and these were people who did not understand Spiritualism. I hoped that we would keep in touch as the years go by, as friends, because her husband too had had his own confirmation of what she was saying was spiritually true. I believed they had both been on Astral Travel that night.

Most of us go on Astral Travel without even realising it, this is when we leave our physical body and travel anywhere throughout the universe. Sometimes we are lucky enough to remember but most of us can't. How often have we experienced a feeling that we've been somewhere before, you know what's round the corner before you get there; you know what buildings are going to be like, whether its inside or out? Have you ever noticed how your body seems to 'jump' as you begin to relax, normally just before you go to sleep? This is when you're actually returning from Astral Travel. Sometimes you're lucky enough to remember where you've been, normally you've only left your body for a few moments of our time even though it may seem within that dream or sensation (whatever you like to call it) that you've been gone for a long long time. There is no such thing as time in spirit, time is just recognised here on the earth plane, yes we have 24 hours in the day and sometimes we need them, but in spirit you're lucky enough not to be restricted by such a thing. When you go on Astral Travel you can meet friends in the spirit world, you can go anywhere on the planet earth, to the outer atmospheres, to other universes, you can communicate with various people that have passed a long time ago, you can learn so many things, you can actually (with the correct training and with the knowledge) meet our friends off the earth plane and communicate with them through Astral Travel, but what you need to always be aware of is if you go on such travelling somebody else on the earth plane needs to know you do it regularly, you could encounter whilst on Astral Travelling reaching too far, becoming weak and not having enough strength to actually come back, but somebody can with the correct knowledge reach you and bring you back into your body. So think about this and next time your body seems to 'jump' just before going off to sleep and if you're lucky enough to remember where you've been, good. This is yet another area where we must remember to ask our spirit helpers and guides for help before committing ourselves on such a journey, working together and team work is what it's all about.

Just as I was leaving the hotel to start my journey home, I talked to the young receptionist, as I could see she needed help.

I gave her my card and told her how to use it, I said that if at any time she needed to contact me to give me a ring.

Not long after returning from Cyprus, I started having stomach pains and couldn't understand why, I couldn't distinguish between whether the pains were my own or someone elses. The following day I heard my friend Jane (in Germany) had had her baby. This explained the pains I was feeling and she thanked me for all the healing I'd sent her and her baby, the pair of them were doing really well. It's nice when you get feedback like that and a thanks. Sometimes my phone never stops ringing with people that need help or to let me know just how they are getting on. These people ring me from not only in England but other countries as well.

As October came, I decided to start some other groups as well as my Friday night group, as so many people wanted to learn I thought it would be a good idea. So I soon started other groups to get them on the pathway, I hoped to put them where they needed to go, and to teach them what they needed to learn.

On the 11th October, my friend Jean, from Burnham-on-Sea passed away with cancer, right up to the end she'd talk about the spirit world, she didn't seem to suffer and went so peacefully. She was such a lovely lady and I was pleased I'd been given the opportunity to become her friend, her husband Joe was also my friend and I knew I would be able to rely on him and he would be able to rely on me for help in the future, as we had that friendship between us like a bond of Spirit Brothers.

In October, I had problems at work with my health. I'd been a fireman now, for nearly 21 years at the airport, during that time I'd seen many things (I'd also served my time with other Fire Brigades as well). One day, whilst conducting an exercise with breathing apparatus, I developed one or two problems. Within two weeks of that I was finished as a fireman after almost 21 years. What I'd been given had come true, that I would retire as a fireman. I reminisced over the times during the last few years whilst working at the Airport what I'd learned with regards to spiritual contact … as a Healer and learning Mediumship. Me

Myself as a Fireman

and a group of firemen would sit down and talk because we weren't always out fighting fires, (that was very rare in fact!) we would talk of how I'd learnt as a Healer and if I could pick up off any individual, some form of message, at times it would really test me because it wouldn't be done in the perfect peace and quiet which is perhaps the ideal surroundings. It would be done in a busy Fire Station at various times of the day or night, but I did learn a lot about communication, patience and healing whilst serving my time as a fireman. Quite often I'd get a first aid call within the terminal building or on an aircraft, and I would be given spiritually what was wrong with that individual, in order that I could help them as a First Aider not as a Healer.

I waited to see what would happen with me at the airport, with regards to where I went from there. I knew what I wanted to do, but had to wait to see how it was controlled. So, for three months I waited to see where I was led, so I carried on visiting my Churches and having my groups and teachings whilst waiting.

I attended a church in Stockport one night, to watch Medium, who kept repeating herself during every message with the expression 'OK'. Now, if you have ever sat during a message and somebody is repeating something over and over again it annoys you, this did. I was counting on average, how many times the lady was using the word 'OK'. I counted over a hundred times during each message, and to me there was no need for it. There are plenty of words in the English language that you can use. Again, I didn't think she was very spiritual just psychic but the interesting thing that I noticed that night, was that the Church belonged to the World Federation of Healing (as I do) which is unusual because you normally find a Spiritualist Church belongs to the N.F.H. (National Federation of Healers) I continued re-ceiving messages whilst I attended these Churches, telling me that everything would be alright and that changes were going to take place and I would be left with nothing to worry about. They also gave me information about the Spirit World and how people would come to me for help, healing and other things, many helpers would draw close and talk through the different people that I met and I would be able to have conversations with them as I would you if you were with me, and I had gained a great deal of knowledge during the time that I had been involved with Spiritualism. I put so much love into it and I received much back. They always say, whatever you put into anything you will receive back tenfold, and I find this is true with what I've put into healing. I put into it what I want to put into it because I enjoy it. Healing gives me a great deal of satisfaction, I receive a large amount of help, love, light and encouragement from the Spirit World, it's what I do because I love doing it not just for it's rewards. I would encourage anyone to have a look at it and I would never knock anybody for trying. I believe everyone of us is capable of helping people at various times in our lives, how many times do we find we are in a situation at work where someone comes to us and asks us for advice with a particular problem or a bad period which they are going through within their lives? How many times do we find, because we've already experienced it, we can turn around and advise them just what to do? This is what I found has gone on in my life. Sometimes I wonder if I'm fortunate enough to experience certain problems which I've come across within my own life, but when I look back on it know I would say, 'yes, I am', because when I've experienced it; I know the trauma and the pain which I've been through, but this has helped me to understand what these other people are going through, and quite often with healing or talking, you help individuals by just listening to what they've got to say and their problems and by advising them and answering them. This is healing alone. If you look at from when the baby is born and the baby falls or cries the mother or father cuddles it, this is healing. If people were only to realise that they have always given healing to their children throughout their lives. You get a loved one or friend that's got a particular problem and you would normally put your arms around their shoulders and give them a hug, this again is healing. There are so many ways that we can conduct healing, this book could go on forever if I was to actually list them, but I would like you to think about them, of how often you have been in a similar situation when someone needs help or you have been through a particularly rough period where you have learnt from it, and you normally find that if you don't learn from it, that it reoccurs, it's like a circle, it just comes back again, until eventually you learn the lesson.

Early in December Dennis Woods (another good friend of mine that I had been giving healing to) passed away. The church in which the service was conducted was heaving with his friends (he had a very large family who were all very close). Dennis had been coming for healing for a few months, he had cancer. What you need to realise and what others need to, is again, not everyone that comes to you can be healed, there are those that will pass, and like I said before, each time one of them does pass over you feel so much for them, because during the period of healing you become good friends with them, you know what makes them tick and you realise what goes on with their lives, and they become part of you just as much as you become part of them, so when they come to pass, you know they will be happy where they will go, but you still miss them and you still shed tears for them.

Notes and Feelings

CHAPTER THIRTEEN

THE VISITING SPIRIT

I found that my sister and brother-in-law were coming on really well as Trance Mediums within the group, not everyone wants to become a Trance Medium because they feel that they want to go their own way. I've noticed that Trance Mediums have various levels of trance from light to quite heavy, and sometimes when I've talked to individuals that are Trance Mediums, I notice that things crop up that we've talked about while they're under. I believe this is their subconcious that is bringing this in to the conversation when their Helpers are talking through them. I've also noticed no matter what language the individual may have spoken, before they passed in to the World of Spirit, they can now communicate in the language that we know and use. Spirit also have to go through periods of time where they too must learn how to communicate with people on the earth plane, they must learn that they are no longer on the earth plane and suffering the ailments that they would have done whilst here, and, if they chose to return to the earth plane, they could choose who to be and how long they are going to be here, depending on what they may have to learn within this life time, this is what I believe and this is why sometimes, we cannot understand how people come for just a short period of time on the earth, while others remain for many years until quite an old age. They go through different times, good and bad within that life to learn, but unfortunately, what they don't seem to bring with them, is the knowledge which they've gained in previous lives, although they seem, as they go back to the Spirit World, to then put all this information together, because they are then capable of looking at it all. This is my belief, this is the knowledge that I've gleaned as I've carried on along my pathway. I ask you to have an open mind and think about it, if you cannot accept it, OK, look for your own beliefs, this is just one explanation.

December came and went, and at the end of 1991 again I looked back on how, and what I had learnt. I found that my healing was becoming more powerful and I was beginning to pick up more things that were wrong with individuals, I accepted that not everyone could be healed but at least everyone could be helped in one form or another. This is very difficult for us to accept as Healers at times, because we wish to heal everyone, but many cannot be healed. I found that at times I must remove that thought from my mind, that this person must be healed because still I was actually blocking it. I found that different types of music helped different individuals during different situations within healing, meditation and learning. I got the opportunity of trying different tapes of music to see how the individual reacted.

I went through a stage of healing when I touched an individual they would drift off into a deep sleep. It was very peaceful for them, but I asked my spirit helpers to stop this as I didn't want it, I wanted the individuals to be aware of what was going on around them whilst receiving healing. I felt that my clairvoyance had developed very well considering what a short period of time I'd been involved. I could give people short messages that they would accept most of the time. I was determined to work on my clairvoyance and healing, to improve it one hundred percent during the next year. I had made many good friends whilst I'd been involved with healing. Most of them had gifts which they too needed to be able to improve on. I found that I would give them advice and assist them in order that they too could improve the level on which they were working to help others. I was never afraid of helping anyone that wanted to develop, no matter how high they got or how far, it didn't worry me, it was not important, as long as the level they were working on was a spiritual level, where they could reach many people which is what's lacking in this world, too many people are egoistic and won't allow others to develop, that upsets me.

1992 I planned that I would go to Stanstead again early in January for a teaching weekend of three days. I would also have a demonstration to mark my Sanctuary being opened a year. I looked forward to the many things I had planned for 1992 within my Sanctuary and within myself as regards to learning. I still wished to be able to dedicate my life to healing and teaching. I wanted to travel the world, to reach many people and help them. I found that I'd made contacts all over England, in France, Germany, Holland, Cyprus, Australia, America, Switzerland and in Israel already, but there were so many other places left to cover.

Hillary and Allan had a particular problem right at the beginning of the year with their young dog Bonnie, a Yorkshire Terrier. Bonnie actually passed over and everyone was heartbroken because it was a family pet only about 7 years old. When she passed they brought her back to my Sanctuary, we said a few words for her and I eventually buried her in the back garden. I hoped that Bonnie would still join us when we had our circles as she always had done. The same day I cleared my locker out within the Fire Section, 21 years to the day which I'd started, so I won't forget the beginning of 1992.

As teachers we should be open minded to our students opinions and wishes, we should never hinder them if they do choose to go their own way.

Hillary and Allan took the loss of their dog badly, and they didn't return to my group, which was a shame because I watched the two develop into very good trance Mediums within the two years I'd been teaching them.

I invited Dot Matthews down to give me a demonstration for the marking of my Sanctuary being opened that year. Again, everything went well and everyone thoroughly enjoyed it, you would usually find that the problem you had was actually saying goodnight to the people at the end of the evening because it would often be past midnight before they decided they had to go home.

On the 8th January I started my job as Temporary Information Assistant at the airport and I knew this was what I wanted to do for a period of time, and that, for some reason, it would help and teach me many things, but at this particular time I did not know what.

On the 14th January I was informed that Dorothy Gray had passed away. Dorothy (if you can remember) was the lady from Brighton who said that she had waited 24 years to meet me and she'd had some information for me. To this day I've never received that information or found out what it was, but I do believe it was there somewhere. Friends would visit me like Jane and Lynne whom I'd met at Stanstead (Jane now lived in Germany but she was moving to Cyprus and Lynne lived in London). I find that people would come to visit me more now from various parts of the world. Joe had some friends from America who he felt needed healing, so brought them to me. I successfully gave Jack healing and picked up all his ailments including when he first came to my Sanctuary he had no intentions of even sitting on my stool to receive healing. Afterwards I gave him and his wife some clairvoyance about their friend in America, and when they got home they discovered everything I had said to them, on their answering machine. After this I received several calls from the chap in America who was distressed, he wanted me to ring him back constantly. What people don't realise is just what it costs you as a Healer and an individual to help people. My phone bill has been astronomical at times where I'd received calls for help on my answering machine from people in need and I would ring them back to help them. It does cost you a lot, I would never charge for healing as I believe it is a gift from spirit in order to help others, if I could afford this I wouldn't object, but I do need money to live. In my Sanctuary I have a bowl where you can put donations if you wish, it will always remain there, as individuals can then decide whether or not they wish to make some form of donation. There will always be a cup of tea after and before any groups that I provide, as I don't think it is just for the 2 hours which a group may take place, that you can actually learn. We learn from one another every time someone has a question, if we can answer it we do, but if we can't then it gives us something to think about and something else we need to learn in order to answer the question next time it's asked. A typical question I find I get asked is about meditation;

Meditation to me is when, for a period of time, I can go within myself; I will either go on a walk, visualize a certain article or just simply drift off along a different pathway. As my groups do the meditation, quite often the biggest worry for most is, did they actually 'pick up' from the world of spirit or did their imagination 'move in' to give them what they linked with? This is very difficult at times for ourselves to interpret. Normally a Teacher that would be taking such a class or session is capable of knowing full well what that individual has used; imagination or spiritual guidance. Definitely, whatever we use in our brain for our imagination is linked with this communication, people tend to worry too much about this, there is no need; in time with the correct training and discipline, everybody is capable of reaching a spiritual level through meditation. The biggest problem most people that have a gift of awareness is, to actually 'switch off'. They need to recognise that they must switch on and off, you need to find the way that suits you best, this is especially important with meditation – look at the best method that suits you, I'm not saying that I know everything, I too am learning, I need to look at everything and turn it inside out to get my answers, it's team work. I ask both my spirit helpers and people on the earth plane many questions to get the answer I'm looking for. Everybody needs to do the same, there's not one of us on such a level that knows it all, yet often we meet these egotistic Mediums and Teachers that tell us they do, bunkum, that's all I've got to say about it.

On the 31st January (which was a really foggy miserable day) I made my way to the Arthur Finlay College in Stanstead. I was really looking forward to it as I had in my memory all the goings on that had happened when I last attended. This time I was to be a little disappointed; when I arrived I found the course wasn't really organised correctly, we were given a time to arrive, which we did, and found out we had to wait 5½ hours until the evening before anything started to happen.

That night there were just two Tutors present, the course should have been run by four well known mediums. There were only six of us on the course that weekend we all came to look at the way in which spiritualism was moving forward, to look at the methods we would use for teaching, how we would change these methods and adapt them to today's way of thinking, but right from the beginning what was obvious to me and the others, was that the tutors hadn't planned anything themselves, total lack of organisation and total lack of discipline, I was very disappointed but soon made friends with the others on the course, Mary Armour from Scotland who was a Medium with very good potential, Dorothy Taylor who was one of the Tutors that had been on my German week (and she was running it again in 1992). Tony, who was a policeman but also a Medium and Eddie who attended Stanstead regular and there were one or two others.

I went to bed that night in the accommodation which was provided. If you can visualize, the College itself is a very old, large mansion type house with many bedrooms, my room was small with a single bed in it and there was no one else sleeping in any of the bedrooms near to me. As I lay in bed, about four o'clock in the morning I became aware of a light that had come into my room, at first I thought I'd left the main light on, but then I found I could not move in any way, shape or form, as whatever had entered my bedroom had completely frozen my body, but not my mind. I felt the presence of something walk from the door to the side of my bed, it climbed over me in bed and laid along side me. I mentally spoke to this Spirit and told them I was not afraid and to please step back a little, to give me some space. I could actually feel the breathing of the Spirit along side me, after a few moments of our time the Spirit left, but returned again at about six o'clock in the morning when the same thing happened. I didn't get any information at all from this Spirit as to who, or what it was, why it was doing this to me I don't know, but I did know it made me think.

In the morning when I went down to reception I explained the experience I'd gone through but they couldn't give me any advice or any information that may help me to whom or what it was. Three more Tutors turned up on the Saturday to carry on with the course, but again I felt they had no idea of what was going to happen from lesson to lesson. We learnt some things and there was a lot of talking but I did expect a lot more that would test us to our limits in order that we may go back to our homes and Sanctuarys and hold our workshops to set out more to help people learn.

I went to bed in anticipation on the Saturday night, not quite knowing what to expect, in a way I was dubious, but I went and as the night progressed nothing at all happened, there were no signs of the Spirit that had visited me the night before. I felt relieved.

On the Sunday morning, workshops were set up to test us to see how we got on, but by Sunday lunchtime the majority of Tutors left leaving one man to look after us on his own. He finally closed about tea time with a question and answer session. I felt very disappointed with this course, but I'd made one or two friends that I looked forward to keeping in touch with and the biggest thing I learnt was to be organised no matter what you do. This was just me on one course, there are many courses to go on at this college which help many many people all over the world, I would still go back and I would recommend you visit the college to see what you can learn as well.

I wrote to the college and explained how I felt about the course. Eventually, I received a phone call from Robert Hartrick this showed at least they responded and were prepared to look at the problems which I'd encountered, in order that it wouldn't happen again, so that they got their own act together to continue the knowledge and the teaching that was possible there.

Back at home I continued my job as an Information Assistant, this taught me a lot, how to communicate and how to address people. I would have opportunities where friends would require readings. One of my friends had drawn on a piece of cloth, a circle in the centre, with lines going out from it. On the end of each line would be a word like 'love' or 'work'. The idea being that the person that required the reading would hold a collection of small crystals up to about four inches from the cloth and then release them, and I would give a reading from wherever these stones landed. I felt, and people agreed that the messages I gave them with such a reading were quite accurate. But I was looking for something more, I didn't wish to use any form of gimmickry or materialistic things when I was giving a message, I wanted to reach that individual without the need or necessity to use such a item (Although I felt this was a good starting point). Many people use various things to give people readings; cards, stones, crystal balls, crystals, etc., but my aim in life is to be able to reach any individual, no matter who they are, without any method other than direct contact with Spirit, and I was aiming to do this. I would start by sitting individuals in front of me for four minutes at a time with my eyes closed (so I wouldn't be aware of who was sat in front of me), and I 'gave off' whatever I could see spiritually or psychically for that period of time. The individuals then would change over without giving me any idea of who they were. This was ideal in group situations of up to eight or nine. Four minutes itself doesn't sound long, but if you give off constantly for that four minutes and work on a fast vibration it's amazing how much information you can give to each individual. I have looked to see whether we need a direct voice response from any individual which we are giving a message to and I firmly know we don't, because we are not linking with that voice who responds, we're linking with the spirit helpers that are actually with that individual, and that is the important area, this is what I'd made my mind up that I would work on as well as my healing in 1992 to see how far I could develop by my own means of communication, with my helpers going along side me and giving me the information that I required from the spirit world. I soon found that I had other groups now starting up, I had to fit these groups in between my shifts that I worked at the airport, but there are ways and means of doing something important. I planned more workshops, not only with me teaching but other people that I'd met who were capable of giving demonstrations and teaching certain aspects of spiritualism. Also, at the early stages of February, I had two good friends turn up, Ron and Joan for healing, originally they had come from Plymouth but now they lived in Wells, and with them, whenever they came, I picked up a famous Healer with the name of 'Ted Fricker' and during the months that they would attend my Sanctuary I got the opportunity of reading books on him and his capabilities as a Healer, how people would go to him in thousands and they would have their instant cures, they would have the miracle healings and each time I would question myself why was it not happening with me?

What we all need to recognize is that it does not always happen like that, individuals come to us for healing which is like a course of medicine, and when that course of medicine is finished the individual has been helped and has normally no longer got the problems, but we cannot guarantee this and this does not always happen, we must learn to accept this no matter how difficult we find it at times, but it is important that we recognize it and acknowledge it no matter how we are committed and dedicated to healing.

I watched as my groups developed each person in their own way, each on their own pathway and I was pleased to watch their development progress. I would learn by the demonstrations that different people would put on for me, with what the individuals that attended actually came for, did they come to learn? Did they come for a message? Or did they just come because they were curious? Each time there was a demonstration

I would learn something from it (and I would hope that the next time I would continue to learn also).

Dot Matthews gave us an interesting talk one night on a spirit operation that she'd received. A spirit operation is just like an ordinary operation except that people from the World of Spirit would conduct it. Our body would actually go through the trauma of a spirit operation as for a normal operation, and people don't recognize this and do tend to forget and try to commit themselves then, to continue their day to day life without allowing their body to adjust to it, this is something we all need to recognize, that a spirit operation can actually remove the trouble itself from our body. There may be signs of a scar then on our skin and yet we have not bled. The obstruction, the object, the problem within our body would have been removed completely but we haven't seen it or we may not have felt it because normally a spirit operation is conducted when we are in a state of sleep, deep sleep caused by no drugs. When we wake up in the morning, we will feel uncomfortable and tired, we may even feel in pain, but we don't know why, but when we come to have our X-rays or medical examinations by the doctors on the earth plane, they are amazed to see that the problem is no longer there, we might just have a scar that we didn't start off with. I would like you to think about this one more because it does happen a lot and unfortunately we don't always recognize that we do need to rest after such a psychic operation.

CHAPTER FOURTEEN

SPRING CLEANING

I was continuing to visit the Churches and demonstrations, again still looking at the way they came across, the way people were dressed, the way they conducted themselves throughout a demonstration, ninety per cent of the time I was disappointed. At times I felt that I was being too choosy and having too high a standard of what I expected these people to achieve, but I don't believe I am wrong, I believe they need to improve on everything they do and the levels they reach in order to help many people.

I would push my groups to the limit at times, I would always allow one of the group to say a prayer at the beginning and another one at the end, within this prayer they would ask for protection, healing, love, light and knowledge. We would try all kinds of exercises to see how far we could actually reach, to see how we could tune in as individuals to whatever was given that night. I was very pleased with the progress of each and every individual that attended the groups. I didn't expect something from everyone every night as I knew some would not be capable of it, but I discovered that I would know if that individual had actually picked up or if they were imagining it. Imagination definitely does come into it somewhere, whatever part of the brain we use for our imagination I feel it has a connection with how we can actually pick up and tune in to the Spirit World. People always say the Spirit World's above, but it isn't, it's actually all around us, it's just like another dimension that is within ours, all the time and what we need to be able to do is to tune into that dimension and be able to give off what we can see, hear, sense or smell.

I gave a demonstration one night on healing and an individual said there was a particular smell from me. At first I was worried because I thought I had B.O. but what I actually discovered was, that whatever was happening while I was giving healing, gave off an odour, not a bad odour just a different form of smell. This can happen to us when we're being used as instruments, not only for healing, but for mediumship as well. Sometimes what we have to be careful of, is the energy we use is not our own and that we are a channel, an instrument to be used by Spirit. When we use our own energy it causes us to feel depleted and worn out, this should never happen when we reach this situation, but being human we can fall into this trap. I would ask you to look out for this and be aware, if you find you are working, regularly feeling worn out and exhausted then look at how you are actually working and communicate more with your Helpers. So many Mediums themselves, don't communicate with their Helpers, they don't actually talk to them either physically or mentally, they just rely on them one hundred per cent for giving information which they then can give off, but I do feel it is a two way system that needs to be used, we need to communicate with Spirit as Spirit needs to communicate with us, we need to be aware that we can ask them questions constantly, but we may not be aware of the answers that we are actually receiving at that particular time, but don't feel let down just continue asking the questions, as one day you will receive the answers when you least expect, again, be more aware.

It is so important that we play our part as well. I've passed comment and I've been quite critical on the Mediums and the various people that play their part in the Churches and demonstrations, but it is also important that we play our part when we go to them, love plays a major and important part of it whilst we are there it's important that we send out our love, love not only to the Medium and the people that are working within the Sanctuary or the Church, but to the Spirit Helpers as well, and by sending off this love to all concerned, you'll feel it come back to you and when that Medium is tuning in and trying to reach a higher level to be able to give a message to someone within the group, your love actually helps them a lot, and they feel it from you. Normally at the beginning everyone is shy and frightened of speaking up when the Medium comes to them but it is important for that Medium that you do speak up and respond. I always like to say 'bless you' at the beginning and I literally mean the words that I say to them, answer clearly but don't 'feed' the Medium. By saying don't 'feed' the Medium I mean that if someone comes to you and says, 'I have this man with you and his name is George', and you reply, 'yes, that's my brother,' or my cousin or whatever you have, you're actually feeding them and you shouldn't, you've actually spoiled it for the Medium. It's that Mediums responsibility to be able to form that link and give you the information, not you give it to the Medium, after all it's up to the Medium to prove survival after death. I personally don't believe that we actually need this direct link of voice between the Medium and the person they are giving the message to, but it is nice for everyone else within that service or demonstration to hear it, and hear how you confirm or deny what they give you. Quite often we have people come through to us, spirit friends that we don't know and the favourites are, 'I don't know them', 'I can't remember them' or 'they died a long time ago'. These are the sort of comments that you get from the people who are receiving the message, but if you find you can't accept them then OK reject them, throw them away, what we often do is store things in our mind which acts like a giant container, with so much information that we're given from various Mediums at various times, but once that container's full we can't take anymore in, so what we've got to learn to do every so often is have a good 'spring clean', and throw away all the material that we can't accept, that we may think is rubbish or immaterial to us. Don't worry if you throw something good away, you will be given it again that will then confirm it to you, so please play your part within that team, it's so important.

Towards the end of March, Shileen travelled down to my home and did me two, one day workshops. She did it on various subjects; Palmistry, Healing, Tarot and Colours combined with healing the people there enjoyed it, not every subject suited every individual that that came, but each and everyone of them went away with some knowledge they hadn't had when they came at the beginning. Sometimes people are afraid of Tarot because they don't understand it, I am not saying that I agree with it, I'm saying that for some individuals it can suit them, if you can form that link with the Tarot Cards then by all means use them, see how you feel and how you are drawn to them, personally, I am not drawn to them, but if it helps you, then good luck.

On the 27th March (which happens to be my birthday), my good friends Mary and Joe Armour travelled down from Scotland to do me a demonstration in my Sanctuary (if you remember, I met Mary at Stanstead) and we got the opportunity during the few days she stayed to have a real good talk about spirit work. We visited many places around Somerset. It was quite obvious that Mary was dedicated to her work for spirit, and I was impressed in the way she was interested in her own progression purely for the help of others. Another thing I admired was the way she travelled from Scotland (a few hundred miles away) and didn't expect a penny for it. During the nights she stayed we discussed how we could improve the standards that are needed in our line of work, basically we felt that the spirit needed to be put back into Spiritualism.

CHAPTER FIFTEEN

FOOD FOR THOUGHT

The weekend Mary was down she did a demonstration for me of clairvoyancy in my Sanctuary. It was well attended and a terrific success. I also asked her, as a favour, to see Non (one of my friends) who was coming for healing if she could give her a reading as Non would often put people my way for healing. Whenever she could Non would attend my groups but due to the demonstrations being at night and her having difficulty driving, she could not always make it. She was so impressed with the reading she had received that she told everyone for months afterwards about how Mary had helped her. It is pleasing when you get a response like this because it shows that someone has reached out and helped at one stage.

At the beginning of April I recognised that I needed a quiet period, and made my mind to go to France again, to work on my book and to see how I would get on. Two days after this decision I was in Wells Church where the Medium Myfanwy Jones was doing a service, she told me that I was travelling to France and I would be walking around a lot, thinking, but it was what I needed. I thought this was good to hear from spirit.

Whenever she was in the area, Tracey (a young girl studying stained glass at Wrexham) attended my workshops and demonstrations, she had offered to design me a cover for my book; I gladly accepted. I had had this feeling from Spirit for over a year that someone like her would turn up to help me. Quite often at times, this is what happens when I need help with a certain problem, someone turns up and helps me with it and this is what Tracey was going to do. She was going to do her bit, and design me a cover for my book based on the experiences which were in it.

Are youngsters today in the spiritualist movement being given the opportunity to learn, to gather knowledge, to take positions within our Churches, on committees? I don't believe they are. The first impression they get when they come into our Churches is important, the way they are greeted because of their age and dress also affects them, the older generation tend to ignore the younger generation, but these are our Mediums and Teachers of tomorrow, none of them should be ignored, just because they tend to dress their way or they are young. They need help and we should be giving it to them in a far bigger way than we are today, we should be showing them the correct way of re-sponding to Mediums from the platform. On how to conduct themselves during demonstrations, on how to send out that love and light that's required to everyone, to show that they too can work as part of that team in a very big way. Perhaps we need to be going back before the youngsters actually come in to our Churches, to be visiting them in their schools and colleges, on the curriculum is religious studies, but is spiritualism part of that study? No, why not? What's wrong with the spiritualist move-ment? Are we saying it's good enough to take part on a Sunday in Church but it's not good enough to be taught in our schools and colleges? Surely interest should be created at an early age, shouldn't we be going out there looking at people and showing them our way and allowing them to come into our movement if they so wish? We often condemn people for coming into our Churches from Psychic Fairs, how can we condemn them when people are not getting the answers they want from us because we are failing to go out there and reach them? People are frightened of religion, as during the centuries it has caused many problems, so many wars, so many deaths, but we should be learning from this and see what we can do as a team to reach these youngsters of today. To answer their questions, to give them what they are looking for, immaterial of how old they are, none of them should be under-estimated or treated badly because they are young but that is what is going on today in our Churches, often they will only come in once because of the way they are poorly treated. If you look at children, how often are they talking to an imaginary friend? They play with them, they share everything with them and yet we can't see them and what happens when they talk about their friend? They are told by the parents it's wrong, they shouldn't do that, its evil and yet here we are with youngsters that have the capability of communicating with spirit quite harmlessly, quite peacefully but we are condemning them for doing it, this is done quite often by the parents because they don't understand the capabilities of the youngster and are frightened because they do not know. Look at it and watch how many times you can actually relate to somebody you know going through that particular experience, where their children seem to have a friend for several years and then the link seems to break, the communication as the child develops more in to an adult is lost, this may be because children become more materialistic when they grow older and their minds become clogged with day to day problems. How many times do we see materialistic things affecting all of us? How many times do we put materialistic things before our spiritual ones? Yes we do live today on this planet, we do have to eat and sleep and go through our normal, routine things, but we should be able to find a happy level of materialistic and spiritual where we can live our life happily.

Some youngsters are gifted right from birth by seeing or communicating with spirit and they never lose this gift, they come in to our Churches, 15 or 16 years of age, they can probably see or communicate far more than we can but do we recognise it? No, we reject them immediately because of their age and dress, we have all gone through periods of our lives when we dressed to suit ourselves not to suit our elders so we all should understand. We need to be able to communicate more with the youngsters of today, to recognise them and respect them in their own way, the levels of spirituality will differ within each and everyone of them, the levels of communication that they are capable of, but they come to us for advice, for knowledge to improve this communication they've had with spirit but we have failed to give it to them. Why don't we wake up and recognise that we can and should, all work together immaterial of how old we are. Often our own mediums seem to 'lose it' when they get old, but they don't lose their respect from one another but the youngsters don't get the respect they deserve too. Think about it.

In May I travelled up to Essex again to see my friend Shileen and I did a demonstration in a Sanctuary one night with a lady Medium, it proved very effective to mix both a demonstration of clairvoyance and healing together. We see healing demonstrated in our Churches very little and I wonder why, because to me healing is the greatest gift of all; when one human being can help another human being to get better. But for some reason we are lucky if we see it once a year. Healing is carried out in our Churches to help individuals but we do not see it as a service or a demonstration, why not? If you belong to a Church or a group why don't you ask for a healing service and see what you can get out of it. After all there are so many people out there who need our help today, let us give it to them.

Another thing that we need to recognise within our own development is that we go through quiet periods at certain times, this is where we don't seem to be able to get anything at all from spirit. Quite often this is when our helpers are moving away and letting new helpers and guides move in, as they too learn from all of us, they also move on to other areas to learn. Sometimes this quiet period can last days, weeks or even months. Quite often I experience this myself and think they have left me. Please recognise this, as this too is important in our development.

A friend and Medium Malcolm Janes contacted me to explain

what he had been recently picking up; it was a young girl who had been murdered some 14 years before that had lived in the area of Exeter. Many of the things that he had been picking up were very interesting and as time goes on I intend to find out how accurate he had been with what he was saying to me about this particular girl. They had never found her body but Malcolm claims he knows where her body is; they have never found anyone for the murder and we believe that by linking all the information together there could be a clearer picture formulated to help the people who are looking for the murderer. He had met one particular man who was obsessed with finding the murderer of the young girl, he was (in my opinion) blocking anyone seeing the truth, not intentionally but his obsession had become so strong he couldn't see 'the wood for the trees'. Malcolm was due to meet this man at the place where he believed the body was, on the Friday, but I advised him quite strongly, not to meet him as the circumstances and the time was not right, Malcolm took this advice and the man became very annoyed because he wouldn't meet him but he would have to wait until a later date to have things sorted out.

The day afterwards another man turned up at Malcolm's home who was what I call on the 'dark side'. Malcolm wasn't aware of this when he let him in, this man informed him he was a white witch and wanted him to join him. Malcolm immediately refused – I've warned you before that you need to know that these people are around. Malcolm was very concerned for quite a few days after this over being approached by such a man.

I did another demonstration in the Pyramid of Friends. So many different types of people attended; some were quite interested, some were just curious, and a few were there because there was nowhere else to go. There were a few of the old faces that were there the first day I ever did a demonstration. My demonstrations change as I develop, I try to make people aware of what I have learnt in order that they too may pass it on. I always have to cater for the type of group that I have in front of me no matter where I am, because each one is different.

I made my mind up in May that I would finish my employ-
ment in October and dedicate my life to healing, teaching and
learning. As I know we can learn for the rest of our lives. There
is not a single day where I don't try to learn something, no
matter how small it might be, with the idea then of passing it on
to others so they too may be able to use it.

On the 22nd May I eventually travelled to Scotland. My
friends, Mary and Joe had invited me up for the weekend. When
I came to look through my messages I realised not only had I
received this journey at Stanstead that I would travel to Scotland,
but I had been given it various times by many other Mediums.

Whilst in Scotland I had the opportunity of visiting various
Churches and making new friends, talking and discussing about
healing as usual. I find I do that wherever I go; I had a lovely
weekend, it was filled with sunshine from the people I met and
the feelings I got from them and from the friendliness and
spirituality of Mary and Joe.

I came back from Scotland feeling that my batteries had been
charged and I was ready to carry on. I spotted an advertisement
in the Psychic News for Healers and Demonstrators to tour in
America, I applied for the position to see what I could learn out
of it. But up to date, I've had no response.

Malcolm and his wife Sheila contacted me again to tell me
they were having problems, they felt generally run down as if
something was draining them so I told them to wear a cross.

People often think it's a myth that a cross can protect you
from evil, but I can assure you that's not the case. We always
underestimate the strength of a cross, the powers it has within it
and you find if you come in contact with anything on the dark
side the cross will protect you, all you simply do is hold it up
from around your neck (if that is where you are wearing it).
Sheila went to buy a cross from the local jewellers in Taunton, an
assistant picked up the one she chose and as she was holding
the chain up (with the cross attached) it suddenly flew off the
chain and under the counter where it was just impossible to get
at. Everybody looked shocked and couldn't believe such a thing

had happened with the necklace. She never said anything to the assistant and continued to buy a different one, both Malcolm and Sheila now wear a cross all the time, for protection, protection against the dark side which was obviously trying to move into their life.

A person from Cyprus rang me one day (it was the young girl that was on the receptionist desk). She contacted me to tell me that she had been using my card in Israel, not for healing and help as we would suspect but her and her husband were in a Casino and he was losing, so she decided to use the card to see what happened; the response was that they won. She never told me how much but I don't agree with people using my card in this sort of manner. That is not what it is for, my card is for help and healing and if you need help to learn then you just ask and you will be given it.

Malcolm had been contacted by a reporter that wanted to do a story on the murder, but soon after he was contacted by the original man who told him the reporter had completely vanished; all his clothes and everything was still at his flat but there were no signs of him and nobody had seen him for many days, perhaps he had got too close to what was actually going on with the death of the young girl, as Malcolm believed witchcraft was involved in quite a big way with her murder, as he had picked that much up.

NOTES AND FEELINGS

CHAPTER SIXTEEN

AN INSTRUMENT FOR SPIRIT

I find that my many Helpers and Guides teach me so much, I want to learn and there are not enough hours in the day, this is one of the reasons why I have decided to finish my material- istic work completely to concentrate on healing and teaching.

I attended a talk one night at a Sanctuary in Brislington which my friends run, the talk was on U.F.O.'s, I find it a very interest- ing subject. The chap that night talked for two or three hours and gave us plenty of food for thought, allegedly, there have been 12 different types of U.F.O.'s already discovered on this planet. In America from the 1950s there have allegedly been U.F.O.'s captured and kept on certain American Airbases. There have also been flying saucers, which are regularly reported and again, allegedly, the U.S.A. have got one or two with which they are experimenting on, but for some reason the Americans fell out with the aliens, what I could not understand is with all the modern technology why there are no recent photographs of any kind. Is this because the Government stops this sort of photo- graph from coming out in fear of scare-mongering? I do believe there is something else out there of a far greater intelligence than us.

I remember meeting a young man one day in Watford and he discussed with me his dreams of U.F.O.'s, whenever he has a dream he has to contact a certain department in the Government, they then send someone out to interview him about it, then they also send out another department to interview him and if he has done any drawings they take them away to study, his drawings are not very elaborate and not as I first envisaged, more child-like, even though this young man is about 30.

I believe there is so much more we can learn about U.F.O.'s. I think they are around and are linked with many things that happen on earth. But who are we to know at this particular time just what to expect for the future? Because the future is all of ours. All of us will share it, live in it, grow in it and experience many things together, but that is another story.

On the 19th June I travelled back to France. I had made my mind up that I must have several days on my own, so I made the necessary arrangements and travelled there. As I drove down the long straight drive way to the farmhouse I wondered what my stay would bring this time. It was as if I was going to another world. The hedges were way overgrown and I noticed as I approached the farmhouse that the grass was so long it was as if it had remained untouched since the last time I had been there. The farmhouse is situated some four or five miles from the nearest village. There are no houses anywhere around and the house is only used occasionally, all of this gave it a deserted feeling.

I found I had difficulty communicating with people in the local village because I cannot speak any French at all and the French people I had met so far could not speak any English. So, the house allowed me my solitude and it allowed me time to work on my book. I had eleven days there without any form of spiritual experiences at all. Because I believe that I needed that break from Spirit which they understood, as Spirit too needs that break from us occasionally as well. So they gave me peace to work on my book, which allowed me to think more clearly and to use my mind to study various things whilst I took the opportunity of peace and tranquility which I found at the farmhouse. I know I shall go back again and each time I go it will be different, I have only noticed the odd occasional spirit walking around whilst being there, I am never frightened of being in such a place on my own as I know that I have my protection, and my helpers are always at hand even though I may not be able to see all of them.

On arriving back home from France I received a phone call from Shileen asking if I would go to help her sister's baby. His name was Luke, and he was only six-months-old. He was suffering from leukaemia. At that time he was in the Great Ormond Street Hospital in London.

I made arrangements to go and visit Luke the next day, this gave me just 24 hours to get straight since returning from France. For some reason within my mind I knew I had to go to Church, I found a list of Mediums that were appearing at the Taunton Church (based in a Quaker Hall), so with my friend Joe, I made my way down there. The lady Medium appearing that night was Jean Hole, she was a jolly lady with striking black hair and glasses, and I knew the minute she walked into the Church that she would link with me to give me a message. The service soon got on its way and sure enough the first message she gave within her clairvoyance was to me, the contents weren't really important at that time, but one thing that struck me was what a fast vibration Jean works on, very soon she had covered some 15 people that were in the Church; going to each one with proof of survival, and evidence within her message which they could relate to. When the service finished we had a chat and eventually we went back (with her husband Mike) to their home in Taunton, where we talked to the early hours of the morning on spiritulist work in general; the way the movement was going and how she saw her future. I found that we got on really well and it was nice to meet such pleasant people as Mike and Jean. It wasn't until gone one before I arrived home that morning and with a early start to London I ended up having four hours sleep, and I made my way eventually to Great Ormond Street where I met Pauline, Luke's mum. She took me to meet Luke, and what a beautiful baby he was, there was so much there, so much spirit within him, with beautiful big blue eyes. I gave Luke healing just by sitting him on my knee, I felt he needed so much help and energy for what he was going to have to go through with the treatment he was receiving for his illness. Pauline showed me around the other wards to see the different children that were in, with their various illnesses and ailments. I found that whenever we went into a ward or cubicle to see the children (who normally had their parents with them), all I needed to do was talk, I didn't have to physically touch any of them and I was still sending healing out to each and everyone that I met. Pauline passed comment on how the children changed in temperament and sometimes even in looks, she called it fantastic to watch as the children changed for the better. I ask you that when you start sending out healing can you please remember all the children in hospitals like this one who are suffering from various ailments. There are so many kinds of illnesses that we don't think of, it made me realise how lucky I was that my family and I are all in good health. It gave me

Great Ormond Street with Pauline and Luke

alot to think about, that day in Great Ormond Street, as it's when you are in a situation like that you realise just how many little children are suffering in this world, even in our own back yard.

My work didn't finish that day as when I caught the coach to return back home I met a man I'd not seen for a few years and we talked for all the journey; he too needed help and I found I was able to answer many questions that he had, about what happens to us when we pass, he had one person in particular that kept coming back on his mind the same date each year and I was able to pick up that this lady had passed, and on a particular day she was making him aware of it, I was able to give the ages of both of them, and the time they were together, this proved to him that there was something else to life further than what he knew about. I came back home that night with a terrific feeling of achievement but within the same breath I knew that all the children in that hospital were really ill and needed that extra help.

I found there were many jobs at home that I needed to do and, with my friend Joe, we managed to fit various lights outside the Sanctuary and in the garden to give it an even more tranquil effect than there normally was. On the Sunday night I watched Mavis Pattilla do a demonstration of clairvoyance at the Blue Cross Church, whilst there I met a friend from my course at Stanstead, in January, and she surprised me by telling me that the words I'd used at Stanstead, 'we should never underestimate anyone', were now being used all around the country by the tutors that were there at the time. This just goes to show that you may only say a few words without even realising and they can travel a long way.

Jean rang me again the following week, to tell me that they had been offered a cottage in Devon to turn into a Sanctuary. We talked about it and both agreed it would be a good idea; many people would benefit from her opening a Sanctuary there. My friends Ron and Joan were still coming for healing as Ron was due to go into hospital shortly to have an operation. A friend of mine, Non, also introduced me to a nice old lady called Eva who lived very close to her, she had just lost her daughter a few weeks previously, Eva's daughter was about 60 years of age when she passed so I had gone to talk to Eva and give her healing, she related an experience to me of when she was a young girl and hadn't been married long; Eva and her husband had bought a site to build a bungalow on, in the Birmingham area, they didn't have much money so they tried to do a lot of the work themselves; and after a week of hard work digging the foundations, they had not got anywhere at all; as fast as they dug they were flooded out, and she and her husband could not find any signs of where the water was coming from, so in desperation finally on the Friday night she said a prayer, it was quite simple,

'oh God please take this water away',

within minutes of her saying this, all the water had gone out of the foundations and they didn't have anymore problems with it. This lady now was approaching 90 but she had never forgotten that and she would listen to what I had to say about spirit communication; her husband had passed a few years previously and now her daughter who she was very close to. She was lost, as so many of us are at various times in our life and she needed help, I know that my helpers gave her the help she needed. She continued to come for healing and to listen, each time she would have a few questions that she needed answering, again how often do we have questions we need replies for and find it difficult to get somebody to give us the answer we're looking for, even though it may not be what we expect?

Dot Matthews was down again on the 11th July to do me a demonstration in my Sanctuary. This time I found many people turned up that I didn't know; word was beginning to get around. My Sanctuary was only small and it soon filled up, quite a few of the people present didn't know much about spiritualism or mediumship at all but Dot reached them and showed them how she worked; she gave them something to think about and they all went away happy that evening. She served Bridgwater Church the night after, it amazes me at times how she goes on, how much work she can do without it affecting her own health. Dot's daughter had been seriously ill for a long time and many prayers

Corner Cottage's Garden

were being said for Ruby in various Sanctuaries and homes around the country asking that she got the help she needed. She'd had a growth of 28lb removed from her tummy and at this present time she needed everyone's prayers to help her get over the major operation she'd had, this obviously played alot on Dot's mind but it did not effect her work despite her worry she came over like a true professional showing that the training and discipline she'd had was paying off with her dedication now.

Tracey and myself were working quite alot now on the book; looking for ideas for the photographs and illustrations which were needed to go in it. We'd also go through the book checking it ensuring that it came across OK. Tracey was on holiday from college so she had a few days to spare which we both found we needed to go through the manuscript.

On the 22nd July I had a pleasant surprise, I received a gift of some 30 hymn books from a Church which had just renewed theirs. I was so pleased about this because I felt that I needed them for some reason, as we had tried various hymns and singing within the demonstrations in my sanctuary and each time it somehow hadn't worked.

On the 25th July I got the opportunity to travel down to Devon with Mike and Jean to look at their Sanctuary. There was obviously alot of work to be done there but you could see what a coat of paint and a bit of love would do to the building, outside the house on a plaque were various emblems and symbols with the date underneath them. I asked Jean to try and take a photograph of it or copy it as I knew sometime in the future she would be given just what these symbols meant.

Afterwards I travelled back to Weston-Super-Mare to see Billy Elton do a demonstration of clairvoyance; in an hour that night he reached 29 people by giving them a message. He and his friend Cliff came to stay with me for a week and one evening we were talking when he told me about a book that had been written with his help by a scientist called J. E. Best. The book itself was called 'Link and Communique'. Billy had sat in trance and talked to Mr Best and given him some of the information he needed to put into his book. I haven't had the opportunity of reading the book yet, but apparently there was a female scientist known to Mr Best who had recently passed to spirit, and the book, is all about spiritualism and communication from these scientists' points of view which again, will cater for the people who don't think the same as we do. Billy again served a Church on the Sunday morning, giving 14 messages. At night he did yet another service reaching many of the people that were present. His work didn't even finish there, on the Monday morning he went and did 5 sittings in the Church. On the Tuesday night, Billy did a demonstration for me in my Sanctuary and this is where my hymn books came in; Billy requested that we sang a hymn before we started. I didn't expect the singing to be a success but we sang and it felt like the roof was being lifted. There were 29 people in my Sanctuary that night and Billy reached 24 of them. At the end he went into trance and gave us an address, it amazes me how he comes across and works so well at his age; again discipline and dedication have obviously played a major part in the work that Billy does. When you watch older Mediums work like Billy and Dot you see how the dedication, discipline and training pays off by both the standard of messages and the length of time they can carry on for, the younger type of Medium that has not carried out this formal training would soon fall by the wayside.

Whilst we are being used as an instrument our body should not be physically affected, but some Mediums do not recognise and acknowledge that they are using their own energies and this does seriously effect their performance, Mediums like Billy and Dot are few and far between which is a shame because we should all be able to reach their standard. On the Wednesday night he served a small Church in Taunton, again he gave over 20 people messages, that night there was no stopping him! He just keeps on going.

On the Wednesday Ron went into Winford hospital to get ready for his operation. Following that on the 30th, Jean and Mike came up to my Sanctuary so we could share the afternoon together, Jean told me she did what she called postal readings; which is when you send a picture of yourself to a Medium who would tune into it and give a taped message of what they picked up and then send it back to you. She brought one with her that day to show me how she worked and I sat with her in my Sanctuary as she tuned in to the person on the photograph to give them what they needed at that time. I was very impressed with the way that she worked, she was so dedicated within herself and worked on a very fast vibration so in the 25 minutes that she would put on a tape, she would be constantly talking and giving information for that individual who had sent the photo in. Again it is recommended that the photograph you send in is of yourself. I hadn't seen this done before but I had heard of postal readings, again, it's another way of tuning in with spirit, we must always recognise that we are just an instrument for spirit immaterial of how we work, and this was another way in which we could be used that Jean was showing me. At some time in the future I will get my group to try it to see what we can achieve.

Ron had his hip revision operation on 31st July, he seemed to be going on very well, the healing that he'd been receiving for a period beforehand definitely helped him.

On August 3rd a young man called Graham turned up at my Sanctuary requesting help and healing, he was suffering from tinnitus which is when you have a loud ringing noise in your ear. There is apparently no cure for this and so many people suffer from it. It effects the person both physically and mentally. Because of our lack of knowledge about this ailment we fail to realise the agony the people who suffer from this go through 24 hours a day. The same day Ron was out of bed after his operation, and within a few days was walking with the aid of a walking frame.

Tracey was still coming to my home regularly and we were working on the book every hour we could, it was beginning to take shape, we never realised there were so many things we had to take into consideration when putting a book together.

My friends, Jane and Hazel from Cyprus rang me on regular occasions for a chat or if they needed help with a particular thing. It was funny how they were both on the island and they are so far away, yet they seem so close when we talk on the phone. I found it was so easy to tune into Hazel, even from that distance. My helpers would give her the information and the help she needed at particular times. The young girl had so much work to do in her normal life that she too found out that there were not enough hours in the day for her to cope with the many problems she was given whilst working there. Jane was now working in different areas communicating and contacting many people by helping them, by giving them readings and by talking, and giving healing. She was discovering herself and how her talents were now being put to more use on the island of Cyprus.

People were beginning to turn up at my groups and meetings that I didn't even know of, one girl turned up all the way from East Sussex with a few of her friends that live locally. On Tuesday 11th August Ron came out of hospital, I visited him there in the morning and he was let out in the afternoon. He told me he'd been covered in shingles whilst in hospital which had developed in to sores, but he did not suffer at all with them, the nurses couldn't believe it, how he hadn't felt any pain with his sores or how quickly he was being allowed out following his operation. He is of course taking his time as the doctor told him to and resting as he wasn't a young man himself. This is just another way I feel that healing helps, it prepares you for such an operation, it allows you to have that extra help and energy at a time when you need it for what you are going to go through, as Ron had needed it before he went through his operation.

On the 12th August Jean contacted me and asked me if I would do a healing service at a Quaker Hall in Taunton, I was pleased to accept. I had friends from Yorkshire contact me, Bob and Alice Hudson to tell me that they were coming down in September and would like to come and talk to me. Sandra also called round from Hastings, people were beginning to appear from various parts of the country to talk and receive healing or talk about spirit work.

On the 13th August I received a phone call from a friend of mine in Bristol called Elaine, she had been contacted in desperation by a man who's mother was apparently having problems in her home and she believed spirit were connected. So I arranged to meet Douglas on the Friday night in Bristol. When we met he took me around to his mum's house (which was an ordinary home on an estate in the Knowle area). He told me that his mother had been seeing spirit during the night, she lived on her own and was quite elderly and they didn't know what to do, they'd been to the doctors, they'd had a vicar round to bless the house, yet his mother was still seeing these spirit forms, he said in desperation they'd managed to find my friend's number and contact her, he said he'd looked through all the yellow pages and the phone books and there wasn't anything in there for Healers or people who could help them in circumstances like this – perhaps this is something else that we need to look at, after all, where do you look – under 'E' for Excorsist!? I told Douglas I needed to walk through the house to see what I could find and what I could pick up, so I did and sat in the particular bedroom that his mum was having problems in. The room was situated with the bed underneath the window and at the end of the bed was quite a large wardrobe on which your eyes get drawn to look at the grain of wood, you could visualize faces within the pattern of it. The lights of passing cars could have created a shadow in the room which could have been mis-interpreted as spirit form. I could not 'pick up' anything in the house that I felt would be causing a problem. He then took me around to meet his mum who was at his sister's house and I talked to all three of them and we went into what his mum was experiencing in quite a lot of detail; what she seemed to see quite frightened her during the night when she used to see what she believed was spirit, she'd even come out of her house and stand at the gate due to being (quite obviously) scared. I didn't know if it was an illness or she was actually seeing spirit, so I gave her healing and picked up the conditions that were wrong with her which she was suffering from. I talked to her and explained how I thought she could cope with the situation. She went back home eventually after 2 or 3 days and everything was OK for a period of time then she started 'seeing' again, I couldn't honestly say that it was spirit that she was witnessing, I believed it was her imagination and there was a health problem that was causing it. At times we need to be able to look at this and still offer people the help that they need and give them the healing and love and not be afraid to ask them to see a doctor, after all we are supposed to work together in a complimentary way.

One evening I saw Jean and Mike at Church and they asked me if I would open their Sanctuary for them, I was pleased to accept and looked forward to it.

My good friend Mary Armour was touring South Wales doing a Church service or demonstration each day and fitting in readings as well. She did a week of this, touring the area and reaching many people by serving several different Churches. She'd been invited to go to Iceland for 3 weeks but she had to decline this due to her commitments at home.

On the 23rd August I reached the thousand figure of names in my healing book, I'd given healing that day to Ron and Joan in Wells, it was the first opportunity I had of seeing him at his home

from left to right: Jean Hole, myself and Mary Armour

where he was doing very well which I was pleased about. Mary and Joe Armour came to stop with me on the 22nd August for the weekend and that night Jean did a flower sensitive demonstration in my Sanctuary where 25 people attended, each one of them had brought a flower and each one of them received a message from the flower. Jean covered everyone present in just 45 minutes, again she worked on a very fast vibration, hardly having time for breath between the messages that she gave from each flower, but it gave everybody something to think about and I liked the way she worked. She asked me if I would work with her on the platform, that if I gave the address she would give the clairvoyance. I said I would like to do this as I felt we could work well together. Mary and Joe travelled back to Scotland on the Sunday night and I visited Blue Cross and Bridgwater Church on the Sunday also.

Elaine Mole a friend of mine from Burnham-on-Sea brought me a lecturn for my Sanctuary. It fits in so well with the other furniture and I feel many people that talk and demonstrate there will use it.

I rang Shileen to find out how Luke was getting on, she said he had been very ill with the treatment he'd been having, it had really taken it out of him, he had needed extra help that time when I saw him, and he still needs many of our thoughts as time goes by.

My groups were still meeting on a regular basis and the people who attended were developing in their own way, developing their own gifts and I hoped I was helping them to improve the way they came across with the communication from spirit.

On TV and Radio for years now we have seen religious services, we've seen discussions on all parts and all religions but why have we never seen a spiritualist service on the TV? Why have we never heard a spiritualist service on the Radio? Why when you get religious programmes are there no representatives from the spiritualist movement? We could go on forever and a day on this one! Look at it and start doing something about it if you are interested. Start asking your MP's, start asking the TV programmers. The people that organise these programmes for both TV and radio need to hear your voice, need to be contacted by you and then perhaps we would see more of it, we could reach more people, more people could receive help, think of all the lonely, think of all the people in their homes just listening or watching these programmes that could be reached if they too knew about our movement. Maybe people do not get involved with spiritualism because they don't know our movement exists – how would they know, adverts don't explain what our Churches are for.

CHAPTER SEVENTEEN

VISIONS OF ENERGY

I travelled with Tracey to Shileen's home in Essex on the 2nd September, the first evening I worked with Shileen's group; we talked about and demonstrated various energies within each one of us, the group was made up of different types of people, but everyone worked well together and created a fantastic vibration, we all finished that evening full of warmth and contentment. What I found interesting to note was the way everyone greeted each other, instead of the usual smile and 'hello' they gave everyone a hug, naturally I was taken aback by this show of affection, but I was also taken aback by the power of the vibrations in the circle, so I felt this was the connection; we work better when we are more open to each other, we are all afraid of our personal space being 'invaded' but after it has been, we feel far 'closer' to the person who has broken down our barrier making it easier to talk and share our feelings, which improves the vibrations we give out and therefore the energy in the room. The day after I travelled with Shileen and Tracey to a shop in Burnham-on-Crouch where Shileen was working giving readings. During this time I managed to give various people healing who came into the shop. That night we went to do a demonstration at Glenwood using Kirlian Photography. Shileen and Brian had bought this Kirlian Camera, with the idea that it would take pictures of the energy within people's hands and Shileen would interpret the results.

Kirlian Photography was invented in 1939 by a Russian scientist called Semyon Kirlian. He was working in his research laboratory when he accidentally allowed his hand to move close to a live electrode, curiosity overcame him as he received a spark of electricity accompanied by a brilliant flash of light. He experimented further by placing his hand behind a piece of light sensitive paper and on developing the photo, Kirlian found strange streamers like emanations surrounding the image of his finger prints. Inspection of this found each emanation had a different radiation pattern. He looked into it further and then in 1970 Brian Snellgrove explored in great depth becoming the originator of the Kirlian Auro Diagnosis which has now been proved and tested. Kirlian Photography works with the use of a dark room. A piece of photo sensitive paper is placed on the electro plate of the Kirlian Camera then the hand, foot or object rests on top allowing a small electro-charge to pass through the paper for a few seconds, on developing the photo sensitive paper which shows our Auric field of radiation, this energy pattern would change by the different states of our mind. Health, emotions, thoughts, feelings, psychic and spiritual energies both positive and negative attitudes, all have an observed effect.

This night with Shileen, we intended to conduct an experiment that would show us and the people we were conducting it with, how it works and how healing works. A few people had requested to take part in the demonstration, the idea being that first of all Brian would take the picture of their hands before they had healing (I too had my hands photographed before I commenced the healing), each one of the people would then come to me for healing, and then would go back and have their picture taken again to show the difference before and after healing. This went on through the evening and we got through about 10 or 15 people. At the end of the night I had a picture of my hands taken again to show the difference in mine. Shileen then talked to each individual on what she was picking up spiritually from the photos, it was amazing to see the difference in the hands, it was pleasing to see when I talked to Shileen about what she had picked up by looking at the pictures that it was roughly the same as what I picked up with each individual when giving healing.

Kirlian Photography is an area which I feel has not been used to its full extent, there are many variations that we could experiment with, this was just using the hands, and was in black and white. There are cameras that can take pictures of your Aura in colour, your Aura round your body which some people can see without the use of photography. The Aura depicts the type of person you are, any illnesses you may be suffering from and many other areas which a trained Medium can see, some people don't appreciate the value of this camera or the photographs it takes because they feel you should be solely working on a spiritual link, but what I feel you need to recognise is that here is something that you can actually physically see the difference with, you can look at it and then form your own opinion.

I was very pleased with results and I hope at a later date to be able to have the opportunity to conduct more experiments with them.

The day after we all travelled to Great Ormond Street to see Luke, he hadn't been very well now for many weeks and when we got there he was extremely sick. Again, I gave him healing as he needed it, it was almost as if he wanted his batteries charging again, to be able to help him. There were many new children in the wards that needed help, I couldn't make my mind up this time as I went into the ward whether or not the children were receiving the full help I believed they needed. I know today that nurses are really pushed to the limit and they do a very good job, but I felt there was something lacking there that day in the hospital to help these children and I couldn't put my finger on it. Again, I ask you to remember children in your prayers each day as so many of them need our help.

The days sped in September and on the 16th I received a letter from my friend Mary Armour, she informed me that I

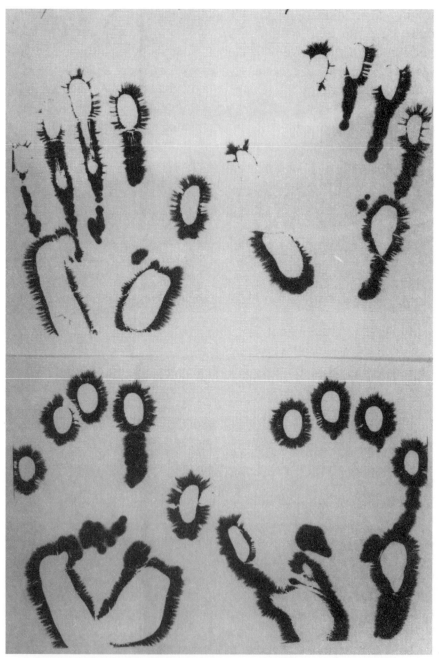

Hands before and after healing using Kirlian Photography

wouldn't be able to do a talk and demonstration in Edinburgh that was planned with her in November, due to the local committee of the Church disagreeing with me doing it because I was English, that there was Scottish Healers and Mediums that could demonstrate up there just the same and they would take offence as I was English. I felt myself we are all supposed to be spiritual and love one another, it doesn't make any difference what nationality we are or what colour or creed, it doesn't effect the work we do. I feel that this particular committee are failing in their responsibilities to recognise this. It did upset me but it won't stop me from continuing my work.

That evening I did my healing service at the Quaker Hall. I managed to give 11 people healing during the service, again I was invited back to do another one in the New Year. I felt that each one of the people there that night benefitted from my helpers giving them healing which again is what is so important, to help one another.

September 19th, nine years and a day to the day Phillip passed, who would have dreamt all those years ago that I would be doing what I'm doing today and enjoying it?

My friend Tracey and myself travelled down to Devon as I was to open Jean and Mike's Sanctuary (along the edge of Exmoor), some sixty miles away. We arrived at their house which was painted salmoney pink. As we walked into the kitchen (off the drive) the atmosphere met us, so strong and powerful that day. The views from the windows were fantastic, you see all over the hills and valleys, it's as if it's all their garden, the fields were full of wildlife, at one point we watched deer grazing. Their Sanctuary is set off the kitchen, this was painted blue with a blue patterned carpet, the chairs were arranged that day in such a way that people could sit comfortably side by side. I felt so proud of being asked to open their Sanctuary because I knew how much work Jean and Mike had to do there, not only with teaching but many other areas. Jean also had music playing, there were various pictures hung on the walls of scenes that depicted their beliefs. These were often gifts that people had given them thanking them for their help. Very soon the guests began to appear, these people had travelled from all over Avon, Somerset, Devon, Cornwall, Plymouth and London, all around, and the thing that was quite striking from the beginning was each one of these people that Jean and Mike had invited to their opening were genuine people. They were all interested, people who were capable of doing work for spirit. There was only a couple of them that really knew where the Sanctuary was in the house as they hadn't been there before, and that evening when we were ready to go into the Sanctuary, Jean and Mike opened the doors and welcomed each one of them into their Sanctuary with a smile, hand shake and that friendly welcome as people sat down. We opened the evening with the hymn 'The Lord is my Shepherd', I said a prayer, Jean spoke for just a few words although tears were streaming down her face as her and Mike had welcomed the people with tears of joy and love and everyone could feel the atmosphere in there, it was electrifying. I started talking to the friends that had gathered about spirit work, what they could do to help themselves and help others, their own capabilities, and you can tell when you stand in front of a group whether or not they are accepting what you're giving or talking about or rejecting it. Spirit makes us aware of the people that are listening and they all were listening in their own way. Jean and myself had decided to do a joint demonstration; I would give healing to someone for just a few minutes and then Jean would link in and give that person clairvoyance, we would rely on our helpers to make us aware of who we needed to bring out from the audience, and this worked very well that night. We decided that we would only do it for an hour, there is no need to say that there was a clock in front of us, or we were running out of time or our power had gone (as often the excuse is from our Mediums and our workers on our platforms). We were not using our own energy we were not using our power, spirit was using us, the power then would be endless. We decided we would demonstrate for a period of time and then it would finish because everyone then could have their refreshments. We reached about 12 or 14 people that night with healing and clairvoyance which was enough and we closed with the hymn 'Open my eyes that I may see' and the singing in there was terrific, I honestly thought the roof was going to come off, it was so strong and powerful, everyone enjoyed it. We took the names for our healing books and we got some 76 names that night which may not seem a lot to you but that is a lot of people that need help. The evening continued, throughout the house, we all talked and many questions were answered from the things we talked about during the healing and clairvoyance. Questions that often people don't get the opportunity to ask. The evening didn't end until well gone midnight, and everyone left happy and content after enjoying a wonderful evening where they also learnt a lot.

I too learnt something that night; as the service began the nearby Church started tolling its bells, it wasn't until after the service that I remembered a message Dot had given me a year previous that I would hear bells, but I translated the message to mean spirit bells, this wasn't so, it just goes to show how we can interpret something the wrong way ourselves and until the event happens we do not realise how wrong we are.

On Sunday 20th September Jean and myself went to Barnstaple Spiritualist Church, about 30 people attended and Jean and I took the service, with Jean doing the clairvoyance and I opened up in prayer and gave the address and reading. It was nice to feel the warmth from the people during the service, to see their response to what we had to say, afterwards we stopped to talk to some of the people in the congregation and again I felt we made some new friends.

My good friends Bob and Alice Hudson turned up on the 22nd September, they travelled down from Yorkshire to spend a few days and during those we spent many hours together talking about healing and how we could reach the people that needed help. Towards the end of the month Dot came down to do a demonstration in my Sanctuary for the weekend, whilst down she also served the Blue Cross Church. The night of the demonstration at home over 30 people turned up to watch and listen to her, she reached out in such a way that night she touched everyone of them.

Jodie and her Mum came who had never been before, and afterwards whilst chatting to them I soon discovered that Jodie was experiencing a problem with Spirit, this was causing her mother great concern. What was happening to Jodie was she could see a male spirit around her a lot of the time, even when she was driving she could see this man in the mirror, no matter where she went the spirit was always with her, this caused great concern to her mother and Jodie as they didn't understand why this man was constantly with her. This was the reason they came to my Sanctuary that night as they needed to find someone to explain to them what was happening. So I proceeded to give both of them healing and afterwards I tuned in to the spirit himself whom I discovered was called Albert. I then continued to give a description of him to her and her mother, soon they realised that the man I described was Jodie's grandfather, although he was not the same as she sees him around her, but my description matched a photograph of him which Jodie had been looking at only a few days before. He was acting like her guardian angel to give her the love and protection she needed at that time, there was no way he would let anything harm her. I told her just to talk to him either physically or mentally, asking him just to step back to allow her breathing space. When Jodie and her mum left at the end of the night you could see a vast difference in the pair of them just as if a terrific weight had been removed from their shoulders.

Dot continued to serve Blue Cross Church Saturday and Sunday, again she reached out and touched the people watching in her own way.

On Wednesday 30th September I went with Dot, June and Brian to Cheltenham Spiritualist Church for an evening of music organised by Mike Carter to raise money for that Church. There was a variety of performances that evening with people involved of many ages. 60 people attended and I feel they all enjoyed the evening as much as myself.

We all have different gifts whether it's being a Medium, Healer, singer, musician and it's good if we can share these with others, like during the evening at Cheltenham. It was good to see Mike again and to see all he was doing to help this Church.

In the beginning of October I made arrangements at home to retire at the end of the month to dedicate my life to healing and teaching. The biggest worry I had was where the money would come from in order for me to survive, all my life I'd thought I was going to die at 45 but now I know it's not death as in the physical death but the beginning of something new, a different path that my life will take with spirit guiding me all the way.

I had many good memories of working at the Airport for all these years and I hope I'd made many friends.

As October was passing I found myself counting down until the day I was to finish at the Airport. I found myself preparing for this day both mentally and physically.

Leslie James a Medium from Stevenage came to do me a workshop on Spiritual Development. The people who attended found it thoroughly rewarding.

During the time Leslie was down I was asked to assist her with a family she knew whose son was allegedly posessed by four spirits. So one evening Tracey, Joe, Leslie and myself made our way to their home. They were living at that time in a small flat, on entering we were surprised to see their hallway was full of boxes, it looked as if they had just moved in, we were greeted by the mother and made very welcome, then her son came in, we were shocked, he was only 32 and 6' 3", and very pale looking. I was to later discover he suffered from M.E. and a serious liver complaint, Leslie and myself then went with him to the living room leaving Tracey and Joe with his mother. The living room was again piled high with boxes of belongings waiting to be unpacked, he explained to us that they had been in their flat for 18 months and according to him spirit had not allowed them to unpack these items.

We talked to him for over two hours asking him questions on his situation. We discovered that he hadn't left the flat for more than 2½ months. He said he had four spirits; two male, two female controlling everything he did, even changing his thoughts. He felt there was nothing he could do to stop them. We then gave him healing, where we discovered how defenceless his immune system was, as if it had deteriorated over the years during his illness.

A priest had visited twice to bless him, with a view of exorcising him but hadn't succeeded. During the time we were giving healing to her son, Tracey and Joe were giving healing in a different way to the mother in the room next door. Both Tracey and Joe felt that the problem was not only with the son but with the mother as well, obviously she would be affected by this situation, but I don't think people realised the true extent she had suffered and was suffering.

When we returned back to the mother, Tracey and Joe. I felt an uneasy presence in the corner of the room, watching what was going on. Up to this point I had not been aware of any presences around us. We all tried our best to cure the situation that this family suffered and we now wait in anticipation to hear the results of our joint efforts.

Friday 23rd October will always remain in my mind as this was my final day at work; this was the day I'd looked forward to since I learnt that I could and would dedicate my life to spirit. Although I couldn't wait to leave my job at the Airport. I knew I would miss the girls that I worked with on the Info Desk, all nine of them had taught me so much.

On my last evening of work just before I was due to finish, I was surprised by most of the women whom I'd worked with turning up to say their final farewell. On doing so they presented me with a gift which they'd all clubbed together to buy. This was a Crystal Ball, immediately I remembered a message Dot had given me six months before saying, I would have a Crystal Ball.

At long last the Sunday night had come for me to do the healing service at Frenchay Church. The weather had been absolutely atrocious so I doubted that there would be many present. Tracey accompanied me to Frenchay and we were both

'Bully' receiving healing

highly surprised on entering the Church at how many people were present, there must have been about 70 people, each person was greeted by Jim Edbrook who was due to chair for me that evening, before the service began he said a few words to the congregation about the healing service being the first Sunday healing service in that Church, but more importantly he believed in Bristol. I then proceeded to take the service by opening in prayer and performing in the same way a Medium would, except demonstrating healing instead of clairvoyance.

The service ended a little different to what I had expected. I was asked to bless a small gold cross by a member of the audience during my closing prayer. Throughout the service the Church became hotter and hotter, I felt this was due to the love everyone was giving off. The vibrations in the Church that evening were beautiful, I felt this was also created not by just the healing taking place, but the wonderful voice of a soloist earlier on – everything combined worked in magnificent harmony.

After the service we were welcomed in to 'Auntie Eidas' home (as she lived next to the Church), we were greeted with a variety of refreshments which we enjoyed but not as much as the company.

This was a lovely way to end a period of my life which was no longer part of me. I knew the following day I would wake up fresh and anew ready to begin the first week of the rest of my life as a Healer and Teacher.

As this book draws to a close I wonder what tomorrow will bring. I look forward to the many challenges still to come. As I wake up this morning, the first day of my new start, I know I am ready to go out into the big wide world.

Thank you for sharing with me my Spiritual Experiences.

Bill Harrison

Recommended reading:
The Quiet Mind, sayings of White Eagle
Spiritual Healing, Miracle or Mirage? by Alan Young
I Hear a Voice, a Biography of E. G. Fricker the Healer,
                                        by Maurice Barbanell

Places of interest
Spiritualist Association of Great Britain
33 Belgrave Square
London
SW1X 8QB

The Arthur Findlay College
Stansted Hall,
Stansted
Essex
CM24 8UD

Dennis and Doreen Fare Healing Sanctuary
33 The Park,
Kingswood,
Bristol
BS15 4BL

Thanks for reading this book

If you find it's helped you, I'd like to hear from you – there may be some questions you have, or some names for my healing book, please don't be shy about writing but enclose an s.a.e. I can't promise I will know all the answers to your questions but I'll try my best.

Thank you again,
Take care,
Bill Harrison.

HEALING LIST

HEALING LIST